A small guide
to great music

A small guide
to great music

English version for the first volume of the book series
"Piccola guida alla grande musica"

Rodolfo Venditti

Edition 2018

Rodolfo Venditti was born in Ivrea in 1925. He worked as a magistrate from 1950 to 1993. In parallel to his work he cultivated the study of penology, specializing in Military Criminal Law, a subject he was lecturing at the Faculty of Law in the University of Turin. He studied with special interest the topic of conscientious objection to the military service and in this field he has been engaged for years with the conscientious objectors operating in civil service and with the movements for peace. His passion for classical music brought him - with writings, music conferences, concerts presentations - to disseminate, especially among young people, the taste for that music and to discover the messages of humanity, nonviolence, peace contained in the compositions of the great musicians. Among his most significant publications: *Il diritto penale militare nel sistema penale italiano,* Giuffrè, Milano 1992; *L'obiezione di coscienza al servizio militare,* Giuffrè, Milano 1994; *Giustizia come servizio all'uomo - Riflessioni di un magistrato sul lavoro del giudice,* 1995-2017; *Piccola guida alla grande musica,* 10 volumes, Sonda, Torino 1990-2013.

This publication is edited by Alberto Venditti.

First Italian publication titled *"Piccola guida alla grande musica"*
Ean code: 978 88 7106 687 5 - May 1990
Copyright ©2018 by Edizioni Sonda, Casale Monferrato (AL), Italy
All rights reserved

Table of contents

The book you have now in your hands is the English translation of the first volume of the book series "*Piccola guida alla grande musica*" by Rodolfo Venditti, an introductory guide to the classical music for novices, published in Italy by Edizioni Sonda starting from 1990. I decided to create this English edition in order to reach non-Italian speaking audience, letting more people to get close and taste the marvellous secrets of classical music, through my father's words.

A couple of warnings to the reader:
- all the content has been kept close to the original book, so you'll find – for example – mentions to Italian books in the bibliographies;
- this has been a homemade translation work, so it's far from being professional; many thanks to the friends who collaborated in proofreading parts of the manuscript (Massimo Fenati, Walter Iuzzolino), actually making my translation better.

I dedicate this work I did to my parents, Rodolfo e Luisa (for everything I learned from them), to Eleonora (she is the foundation of my happiness), to Tommaso (he embodies my concrete hope for a bright future), to Margherita and Benedetta (they act as flowers colouring my days), to Maria and Enrico (for the support they always gave to their brother).

June 2018   Alberto Venditti

INTRODUCTION
The meaning and the limits of this book

I

Since I was young, I had a great passion for "classical" music. I had studied - somewhat listlessly - a bit of piano, taught by my mother (who played that instrument very well); later, during the high school, I had studied - with more diligence - the violin. This had introduced me into the mysterious world of sounds and made me appreciate the great music, especially the great pages of violin literature.

I was thrilled to attend concerts to hear great violinists (I remember I heard live Váša Příhoda and Nathan Milstein). The first records I bought were about violin music (the very first one was Beethoven's Kreutzer Sonata, performed by violinist Thibaud and pianist Cortot). One of the favorite films of my youth was *Armonie di gioventù* (original title: *They Shall Have Music*), produced in America in 1936 and released in Italy in 1939: the plot was about an orchestra of young people in financial difficulties that, after various vicissitudes, managed to play with the great violinist Jascha Heifetz, who performed Mendelssohn's violin and orchestra concert with exceptional talent, making that orchestra famous.

Each week I met with my friends in Ivrea, my hometown, to listen to music. We shared our paltry record collections. At that time - during World War II and in the following years - listening to records was quite a laborious operation: there were only spring-actioned record players and 78-lap discs. One side of a record would last about five minutes; then you had to turn the record over, replace the metal stylus, reload the spring by patiently spinning the crank, being careful not to force it too much to avoid damage to the spring. The listening experience was therefore very rough, and today, in the era of Hi-Fi, CDs and MP3, it seems impossible that only a few decades ago we lived at such "primitive" levels.

A great love for Beethoven's music was especially growing in me. That music was telling me many things: it was a message of moral strength, of liberty, of brotherhood, of hard-won joy. Through that music, Beethoven's personality appeared to me alive and fascinating. It encouraged me to learn more and read about it, and I was fascinated about the tormented and strong life of that great composer. The high ethical commitment - it can be said "Kantian" - emerging from his letters and from the outlines of his life, though not flawless, had on my youth, thirsty for great ideals, a very strong impact, a deeply educational influence.

It became one of the focal points of my human formation, in perfect harmony with the Christian message, whose great richness I discovered with joy through the "Catholic Action" youth movement and through contacts with "masters" such as Carlo Carretto, Giorgio La Pira, Giuseppe Lazzati, Giovanni Getto, Don Mario Vesco and many others ...

From Beethoven my interest extended to many other musicians. First Mozart and Schubert, two composers who, despite their diversity in life and musical language, have considerable affinities.

I was then greatly aided to dive deep into the poetical world of Schubert (that finds its highest expression in the Lieders), by the concert activity of my sister Annamaria Venditti, a soprano, whose repertoire included many Lieders of Schubert. I appreciated so much this aspect of Schubert's work that I collaborated with my sister on several concerts, by introducing each Lieder (composed in German) with a brief presentation of its meaning, helping people to better understand and enjoy Schubert's music.

II

The discovery of great music drove me spontaneously to offer others, especially young people, opportunities for approaching it. Thus, since my university years, I began to organise musical events in which I presented the profile of a great musician, mixing my talk with significant pieces of his music played to the audience from carefully selected records.

Those meetings, which took place in the context of the Catholic Action or within the university association named "Raggio Verde" or in colleges, were very rewarding, because I often realized that they constituted, for some young people, the first opportunity to get acquainted with the "classical" music and to open up new horizons: even today I happen to meet friends, or even strangers, who recount those meetings and tell me that they gave them the first impulse to approach the great music.

I tried to convey this taste for great music to my children too. And when my third child was in fifth grade, his teacher asked me to go some Saturday mornings to his class with my record player and introduce some great musicians to the schoolchildern. I accepted. I tried to simplify the speech and the auditions as much as possible, and I realized that the students followed with interest this way in the world of sounds, they were passionate about the lives of great musicians and liked the musical samples I presented them. The method worked, therefore, also with so young listeners.

Later, when my friend Don Michele Do, who - in the Val d'Ayas - was the reference point for various cultural events in the summer, in the 1970s proposed me to set up some music lectures targeted to those who wanted to approach the great music, I accepted. Thus a singular initiative was born , which covered, summer after summer, a rich music gallery, from Haydn to Mendelssohn, from Vivaldi to Brahms, from Bach to Debussy, offering an opportunity to listen to and/or appreciate again immortal scores.

III

For years I have been dealing with the topic of conscientious objection to military service in terms of legal studies. Thanks to these, I often found myself in contact with young people from various ideological standpoints who were going to raise a conscientious objection or were anyway interested in the subject.

Many years ago, attending a summer camp organized by the Turin branch of the Caritas charity, I noticed that among the participants there was some young music enthusiasts. I then proposed to spend an evening with an absolutely free lecture on Beethoven, a musician who was a firm protester against the Napoleonic dictatorship, and who sang of joy, peace and human brotherhood with unmatched strength and conviction. A lot of young people (more than expected) attended the lecture in the evening: there were no signs of boredom; indeed, the interest was high and, in some listeners, very lively.

Since then, such events have been repeated at similar camps. I can't see why a conscientious objector is encouraged to meditate on Gandhi's or Martin Luther King's message, and not also on Beethoven's messages (about universal brotherhood) or Bach's (about nonviolence).

The fact is that young people are sensitive to great music and are capable, today more than ever, of capturing universal messages.

Even among the young "illiterate" in "classical" music, the charm of great music has immediate effect as soon as the conditions of listening are freed by prejudice and distrust. And I am convinced that the poverty of ideals, the conformism of the modes, the automatisms of consumerism, the evasions in "artificial paradises" can be especially defeated by opening up to young people horizons of art, poetry, creativity and presenting authentic values, stimulating ideals, all fields of serious and constructive engagement. "Classical" music is, in fact, one of those horizons.

IV

This book is the result of the desire to further broaden the circle of communication experiences I have talked about, that is to offer to a greater number of people the opportunity to enter the world of great music or, in any case, to expand their knowledge of it.

This is therefore a book that is addressed especially to those who have not yet been in contact with great music or who - having had some first contacts - feel the desire for more in-depth knowledge.

In addition, the author of this book is not a musicologist or music expert. He is a magistrate (now retired), an expert of law who has always associated with jurisprudence various kinds of human interests and, among them, an interest in classical music. He listened to a lot of music and read a lot about it, but he is only a passionate man who tries to communicate to others the joy that comes from great music and from "friendship" with the great musicians.

Getting to know about the lives of the great musicians and reading their writings (especially their epistles) means acquiring a "key" to better understand and enjoy their music. And since they are personalities that were able to express the highest peaks of art and humanity, "becoming friends with them" means assuming and acquiring their own values and feelings, that are an integral part of humanity's most precious ideal heritage.

V

The idea of organizing the vast material I had collected for years and pouring it into a book was a very remote idea, whose implementation lacked two fundamental conditions.

First of all, the time for writing: this was difficult to find, due to my intense work as a magistrate, university teaching, my various commitments with the family and with the conscientious objectors.

Second, an available publisher. It is clear that, for those who have always published their essays with publishers specialized in law studies, it is not easy to find a publisher willing to publish a book about music.

This second condition occurred unexpectedly in July 1989, just after the birth of the Sonda Editions publishing house and their proposal to collaborate. This gave my remote project an unexpected boost. I decided then, very gladly, to devote my 1989 holidays to the writing of the book. And I spent my holidays in Val d'Ayas engaging in that writing (I can say it: full time) and finding in it an ideal opportunity to realize a drastic and complete (so authentically restful) "detachment" from professional work.

It was an exciting experience. Immersed in the wonderful scenery of the valley and the mountains, I focused on a great musician for five or six days: I revisited the material that concerned him, I tried to see things from his perspective, I listened to his most significant music, alternating the drafting hours with the toning mountain life.

When a musician's profile was drafted, I passed it to my wife, Luisa, who - as a painstaking, sensitive and sharply critical reader - gave me her opinion and, above all, referred to her feelings about how easily comprehensible and effective the text was. As this "revision" took place, I was immersed in the world of another musician, quickly rethinking about his life, problems, environment and work.

At the end of my holidays, the general layout of the book was ready. It was just a question of completing, coordinating, fine-tuning. And these tweaks happened in my spare time, between my judicial work and my university engagements. Finally, the first edition of this book was born.

VI

The book is designed to provide the reader with suggestions on how to look into the subject even further. It sketches brief biographical profiles of great musicians and, trying to focus on their personal stories and the individual characteristics of their art, it offers a "grid" to approach pieces of their music. In choosing the musicians, I left out opera composers: not because they did not deserve attention, but because opera contains already in itself the "keys for listening", provided by the story told by the libretto, by the words sung by the various characters and by the spectacular staging. Purely instrumental music is, instead, more "abstract", and thus requires more research and listening efforts to be fully appreciated.

The pieces have been chosen for their specific reference to the composer's biographical events, for their special accessibility for a "beginner" listener, or for their significance in the musical production of the author.

These are brief and condensed suggestions, intended only to offer a "taste" of the music. They could perhaps be a didactic aid for music education; but they do not have this ambition. They only want to intrigue, seed cues, inspire.

I realize that the the listening tips leave out many important compositions and offer, mainly, an incomplete picture of the suggested musical tracks. But it was not possible to do it differently in a book like this; and the reader will certainly understand the reasons for this structural limit of the book.

Besides, for a person who approaches classical music for the first time, I think that it's better to listen to an incomplete passage (and therefore be tempted to know it in full) rather than having an "indigestion" of a whole piece, risking a sort of a "rejection crisis".

Therefore, no claim of completeness. Probably any musicologist will find many defects in this book, for which I apologize in advance, being very receptive to criticism.

I would like to point out, however, a flaw that is certainly absentfrom this book: in the composers' profiles there is nothing, absolutely nothing, invented by me or fictionalized. Everything that is written has been drawn from biographical sources. You might discuss the reliability of some sources: but there is always a source, and nothing is the result of free invention.

VII

The profile gallery contained in this book presents, in chronological order, six "giants" of music: Vivaldi, Bach, Händel, Haydn, Mozart and Beethoven.

In drawing up the profiles I tried to highlight the human notes of individual composers, the spiritual soil in which their works were rooted. While delineating these figures, there is always the risk - especially for those who have learned to love them - to exceed in enthusiasm, to praise them too highly and with vaguely hagiographic tones. I have tried to avoid this risk, but I doubt I've been fully successful. In that case I apologize with the readers, claiming my emotional engagement as an excuse, as that may have involuntarily led me to pour onto the musicians the great love I have for their music.

In the biographical profiles, I have objectively given space to merits and defects. However, I have tried to extract from their "lives" what is possible to grasp as a "human lesson". I am convinced that musicians' biographies contribute, along with their music, to send us a message that can still be humanly valid.

VIII

The book is designed to allow two distinct reading levels. The parts written in a normal font relate to the biographical and artistic profile of the musician. A smaller font, instead, denotes instructions for immediate listening of pieces composed by the musician.

Therefore, for those who have the opportunity, it may be worth a reading instantly integrated with music: yet I realize that such a system, practical and effective at a conference, becomes so much less easily feasible when reading a book (but of course the reader can decide not to interrupt the reading and to listen to music only after completing the musician's profile).

For those who do not have the option of listening immediately or prefer to postpone playing the music track at a later time, the parts in smaller font can be skipped. The profiles of musicians are fully described with the text in normal font, and such a description can itself set new horizons and stimulate sympathy or curiosity towards a particular musician.

At the end of each biographical profile, I thought it would be useful to dedicate an entire paragraph to a masterpiece of that musician. Thus, there's a kind of short "listening guide" of a series of masterpieces: a very basic guide that offers some quick notes to help you listen to a single composition in its entirety. It may be the beginning of a listening method and an implicit invitation to listen to the other compositions of the author.

For those who will want to study individual musicians more in depth, I have provided some essential information on the cataloging of works and the bibliography of each musician, useful for a better understanding of the composer and his music. These are very small notes, suggestions for further reading, which merely indicate biographies and the most significant essays, mostly written in Italian or translated into Italian.

Quirino Principe quoted an aphorism by Hugo von Hofmannsthal, which says: "Painting transforms space into time, music transforms time into space"; and he said that this aphorism expresses a sort of project to transform the world: a project that "exists since the very origin of human communication in terms of civilization". This seems to me a beautiful image that highlights the relationship between the arts and casts a special light on the nobility and the effectiveness of musical art.

IX

While writing (in 1990s) the first edition of this book I couldn't imagine that it would reach later editions. Instead, the readership has gradually increased over the years, and this proves that the book responds to a real need: to offer a guide to know and enjoy classical music, which is often neglected.

From this "surprise", the Italian version of the "Piccola guida alla grande musica" grew with more volumes about other composers and music ages, thanks to the endevour of the Sonda Edizioni, as well as the careful and intelligent collaboration of my wife Luisa, who has effectively filled my many gaps in computer-aided editing.

R.V.

ANTONIO VIVALDI
(1678 - 1741)

Rhythms and colors
in the Venice of the eighteenth century

François Morellon de La Cave: Antonio Vivaldi, *Effigies Antonii Vivaldi*
for Le Cène edition of *op. 8,* 1725.

For a long time Antonio Vivaldi's figure was wrapped in mystery. Mystery about his birth, mystery about his life, mystery about his illness and his death.

It was not known exactly when he was born. It was known he had suffered "chest tightness", but it was not clear which illness it was. He was known to have died in Vienna, but all memories of his stay in Vienna had been lost. Nothing was known about the date and circumstances of death.

It was known that he had lived in Venice; that he had composed a lot of music, mostly fallen into oblivion; that he was also busy with theater; that for a long time he had taught in one of the hospices in the city; that he had been famous as a very skilled violin player.

His nickname was "the Red Priest," because he had been ordained a priest at the age of twenty-five and because he had tanned hair that would justify such a name. The color of hair was, moreover, a characteristic of the family, because even three of his brothers and sisters (all six were sons, three males and three females) had red hair.

«THE RED PRIEST»

Today, it is known that Antonio Vivaldi was born in Venice on March 4th, 1678. In fact, in 1962 a baptismal register was found in which there is a record that relates to him: it indicates the date of birth (March 4th), attests that the child was taken to the church and received exorcisms (i.e. the rites complementary to baptism, provided by the baptismal liturgy) on May 6th 1678, and states that at the time of birth the child had been in danger of life and therefore "had the water" (of baptism) by the midwife. Therefore, since he was young, Antonio had had problems, and this would explain how his life has always been plagued by a delicate health (but there is also the hypothesis that the "danger of life" was caused by an earthquake which would occur in Venice just on the day of his birth).

The surname Vivaldi is a Genoese surname (made famous in the history by the great navigators Ugolino and Vadino Vivaldi); but it is not certain that Antonio's family had Genoese ascension. His father,

Giovanni Battista, was born in Brescia and moved to Venice in 1666, where he dedicated himself to the study of the violin and became an appreciated violinist at the Cappella Ducale. With Giovanni Legrenzi and Antonio Lotti founded a Brotherhood of Venetian musicians titled to S. Cecilia. He was the one to give his son the first violin lessons.

It has not yet been possible to clarify (and perhaps never will) what kind of illness was the "chest tightness" cited by Vivaldi in a letter. Perhaps it was a bronchial asthma, or any such severe and permanent indisposition that would not allow him to walk on foot: he always moved with a gondola or a carriage.

Moreover, according to what he writes in a letter, that "chest tightness" had forced him to give up the celebration of the Mass after just over a year of ordination: in fact it happened many times he had to suspend the Mass because of that illness, and therefore was dispensed from the celebration. Truthfully, gossips were circulating that the young Vivaldi would have been banned by the ecclesiastical authorities to celebrate the Mass because it had happened several times to interrupt the religious function to go to the sacristy to record some musical themes that came to mind and to return then to the altar to continue the interrupted celebration. But there is no documentary track of this.

Whatever the truth is, it is not even clear why Antonio had become a priest. At that time it was widespread to conceive priestly life not as an announcement of the Gospel, as a service to man, as a gift of salvation, but rather as a "ecclesiastical career", a source of economic accommodation and social and cultural promotion. Being a clericus meant having the opportunity to study, in a society where illiteracy and inculturation prevailed, and to gain access to a socially-appreciated "place", enjoying, in addition, economic benefits: hence, the priesthood was directed to people without vocation and driven only by career ambitions or eager for a social accommodation otherwise difficult. It may be that Vivaldi's father started Antonio in the priesthood, essentially concerned with securing a prestigious social status for a disadvantaged young person who could hardly resist the impact of "worldly" professions. On the other hand, it seems that the mother, during the difficult vicissitudes of childbirth, had vowed that if the child had survived, he would become a priest.

It should be said, however, that - apart from some rumors that were originated later by the subsequent frequentation of theater people (due to his work as a composer of theatrical works) - there is no proof that Vivaldi's life was immoral and in contrast to his priestly status. Of course, his life as a musician and theater man put it in the worldly life of that age, a life that was not entirely appropriate to the ecclesiastical condition. But in his life there are no scandalous episodes; and when Goldoni went to visit him, he found him busy with the breviary, that is the "prayer of the hours" which constituted and constitutes a daily commitment of each Catholic priest.

A SCRAPT OF ART TREASURES

The name "Venice" and the word "gondola" evoke a unique and almost magical world. Venice is a treasure chest of art treasures. To say "Venice" means to say Caravaggio, Tiziano, Veronese, Tintoretto, Tiepolo, Canaletto. Venice is the magnificent architecture of San Marco and Palazzo Ducale, is the art of glass and lace, is Goldoni's theater. In music, then, Venice is Monteverdi and Gabrieli, Scarlatti and Legrenzi, Albinoni and Marcello ...

In Venice Andrea and Giovanni Gabrieli, in the second half of the sixteenth century, had experienced new ways with the magnificence of their vocal and instrumental polyphonies using the double orchestra and the double chorus of the basilica of San Marco; and later Monteverdi had lead the vocal polyphony to perfection and had given impulse to the newborn melodrama. In 1637 the first public theater, San Cassiano, was inaugurated in Venice, with a spectacular innovation that brought music and theater out of the closed courtyards and aristocratic palaces, making music and theater accessible to all: a breakthrough in cultural democratization which would have affected taste and musical style. At that first theater some others were added: in the first half of the eighteenth century the Venetian theaters were sixteen, each of which organizing annually about sixty performances, including comedies, concerts and works in music.

Venice was therefore a city artistically very alive, though in serious political decline. In the years of Vivaldi, also Tiepolo, Longhena, Canaletto and Goldoni were active in Venice.

Vivaldi is born and grows in this environment, artistically and musically fervent. It seems that, after his father, he had as violin teacher Giovanni Legrenzi, a great composer and violinist.

In 1703 he was ordained a priest and in the same year he was appointed a violin teacher at the Ospedale della Pietà.

As a first encounter with Vivaldi I would recommend listening to the first movement of the Symphony in C major P 9. We will immediately measure the richness of the themes and colors of this musician, as it is a short, tasty, and pleasing composition.

THE CONCERTS OF THE «PUTE»

The Ospedale della Pietà is, at that time, one of the four hospitals in Venice for teenage foundlings, orphaned, handicapped, illegitimate children. These hospices are also called "conservatori" (from Latin "servare", which means "to hold, preserve, educate"), because in them the hosts are taught in some art, mainly in music. In the Ospedale della Pietà, only girls are accepted: they learn to sing and play under the guidance of teachers; they give concerts that are very appreciated and presented by the chronicles of the time as one of the attractions of Venice.

In fact, the executions are of a high standard. The people affectionately call these girls the "pute" (in the venetian language they just mean "girls"), or even the "ospedaliere"; and as they perform music behind a grate, the popular fantasy speaks of deformity and horror (in fact, some faces were often marked by smallpox, a very frequent illness at that time), in contrast to the celestial beauty of voices and sounds.

Jean Jacques Rousseau, who stayed in Venice in 1743, gives us a colorful description in his Confessions:

«What annoyed me was the grate that let just the sounds pass and prevented the sight of those beauty angels whose sound was certainly worthy. One day Mr Le Blond said to me: "If you have so much curiosity to see the girls, I can satisfy you; I administer the house and I can invite you to have lunch with them". Mr Le Blond presents me one after the other those famous singers whom I did not know anything but the name and the voice. "Come on Sofia": she was horrible. "Come on Cattina": she was one-eyed. "Come Bettina": the varicella had disfigured her. Almost no one was devoid of any serious defect. I was desolate. During lunch they became animated and they became cheerful. Ugliness does not rule out grace, and they had. I was thinking: you can not sing that way without a soul, and they had. Finally, I became so accustomed to their sight that I went out of there that I had fallen in love with almost all those ugly girls».

A beautiful page, for that discovering the value of the person beyond her physical appearance, for that pointing out that "ugliness does not rule out grace."

But in this orchestra there is another interesting aspect that I think deserves to be underlined. Since at that time the profession of instrumentist in an orchestra was forbidden by women, the orchestra of the "pute" offers us an almost unique example of female artistic commitment and shows us - precisely through the level and fame of that complex and the high professionalism of its members - the absurd injustice of discrimination that excluded women from artistic life as well as from so many other areas of social life.

Now let's pretend that we are entering the Church of the Ospedale on a concert day, sitting in the room and looking up at the two stands, protected by wooden grates behind which the orchestra of the "pute" stands. The *Gardellino Concert* (P. 155) of Vivaldi is going to be played. The Concert's soloist instrument is the flute, played by Sofia or Cattina or Bettina... The festive shard of the flute evokes the song of the goldfinch; hence the name of the Concert (goldfinch is "cardellino" in Italian). Here is the first movement, in which Vivaldi gives the measure of the amazing fidelity with which translates into the instrumental music the lively and melodious song of that tiny little bird.

AN EXTRAORDINARY
MUSICAL EXPERIMENTAL LABORATORY

With an orchestra available every day - moreover a ductile, qualified, obedient orchestra as the one of the "pute" -, Vivaldi finds an extraordinary musical lab in his hands. The orchestra, as a whole, is a "tool" of infinite possibilities: a composer can experiment with the most varied combinations; he can try and try again; he can modify and improve a composition. A musician, usually, does that work by using the piano or the violin; it is very uncommon that it has not only a single instrument, but even an entire orchestra, that means an "instrument" very complex and rich in various voices. Vivaldi has had this luck for years, and his musical genius has been able to pull out of

22

it a full satisfaction and, at the same time, a lively stimulus. That way masterpieces of dizzy novelty were born.

Think about the concerts that make up the collections he called *L'Estro armonico*, *Il Cimento dell'Armonia e dell'Invenzione*, *La Stravaganza*: already in the name itself we have the indication (authentic, because offered by Vivaldi himself) about the research for new ways, the creativity in musical solutions, the particular inventive genius.

If we then go into individual compositions, we find that experiments concern all the instruments and their combinations. In the Vivaldi's research, the instrument's tone, the mixing of different voices, the tones dough dosing, the resulting effects, the feelings and the emotions that they can cause are of great importance. In other words: the colorful "palette" of instrumental voices has, for Vivaldi, the same importance as for a painter the choice and use of colors. In fact, the tone of an instrument is sometimes referred to as its "color".

Let's enter with curiosity in this lab. Let's see how Vivaldi explores the expressive possibilities of the bassoon, an instrument that at first glance seems rather awkward and grotesque: let's take the beautiful concert *La Notte* (P. 401) and enjoy the great expressive resources of this instrument that Vivaldi reveals to us by transforming the bassoon in a marvelous evocator of mysterious depths, fascinating silences, inner peace.

Then let's choose another concert that explores the possibilities of an instrument from the register opposite to that of the bassoon: the piccolo, which Vivaldi calls "little flute", with a sharp and tearful tone. It is Concert P. 79.

Then a concert where Vivaldi plays with five different shades: flute, oboe, violin, bassoon, harpsichord. It's Concerto P. 207: let's listen to its first movement.

And again: the mandolin, a very unusual instrument in an orchestra. Anyway Vivaldi uses it: in Concert P. 133 and Concert P. 134. And the list could continue.

The "concerto grosso", developed thanks to Torelli and Corelli, and based on the dynamic contrast between the "concertino" (limited group of instruments) and the "tutti" or "ripieno" (whole orchestra), and on the so-called "terraced style" (alternating fiery and feeble music blocks), comes to perfection with Vivaldi.

If we want to continue our research, we can listen to how Vivaldi employs the tone of love viola, in the first movement of Concert P. 288. If we want to realize how Vivaldi explored in every direction the possibilities of violin and cello, we find a lot of examples in *L'Estro armonico*, a collection including concerts for one, two, three, four violins, for two violins and cello, for four violins and cello etc.

«TASÈ, TASÈ! EL XE UN CONCERTO DE VIVALDI!»

Vivaldi's style is characterized by impulse, rhythm, energy, and exuberant vitality. In his music there is a solidity, a folk health that subtracts it from aristocratic sophistication and which puts it in the immediate harmony with the popular soul.

In the Venetian theaters they did not always listen carefully to what was played or sung or represented: going to the theater was above all a moment of delight, of encounter, of aggregation; people came with food to eat and met loudly, often letting the music go on its own, almost a kind of background to the talk. But when Vivaldi's music was going to be performed, you could hear this exhortation passing from mouth to mouth: "Tasè, tasè! El xe un cocerto de Vivaldi!" ("Keep silent, kepp silent! It's a Vivaldi's concert!"). People quickly made silence and tasted the cheerful Vivaldi's *Allegro* and the sweet melodies of his *Adagio*.

Vivaldi was a composer not only fruitful, but also fast. He wrote music very quickly: he was delighted to compose faster than a good copywriter could copy.

Vivaldi's fame spread, during his life, all over Europe. He traveled not only to Italy but also abroad, reaching Amsterdam and Vienna. His music was printed in various cities, also abroad: Bruxelles, London, Amsterdam, Paris. He was in contact with various princes, from which it received enthusiastic applause. With emperor Charles VI he had, in Trieste, a memorable encounter where the emperor covered him with gifts and promoted him a knight. Of that meeting it was said: "in fifteen days the emperor talked with Vivaldi more than he spoke in two years with his ministers". Vivaldi had illustrious students; he was praised by famous composers; some of his works were transcribed by Bach.

We could now listen to the Concert Op. 3 n. 8 (from *L'Estro armonico*) that Bach will then transcribe for organ. It is also a wonderful Concert for oboe and orchestra (RV 548); the second movement has a palpitating sweetness: in my opinion, it is one of the highest Vivaldi pages. In it the lyrical luster joins a suspended and contemplative atmosphere, punctuated by long pauses alternating with enthusiastic and troublesome questions played by the oboe.

THEATER AND SACRED MUSIC OF MR. ALDIVIVA

Vivaldi was not only an instrumental music composer, but also a composer of melodrama and a theater man. He composed a number of theatrical works in music, and this activity involved him a lot, making him also the manager of his plays: engaging singers, organizing performances, negotiating with theater owners, enlisting musicians, economically managing the show.

She proudly stated: "I am a free entrepreneur, and I fulfill with my bag and not with loans". This meant that he did not borrow and pay in cash. This intense business activity led him to be wary, tense, nervous, unhappy, concerned.

His works were successful. So he was nervous about being targeted in a satirical volume that came out in those years in Venice. The book was titled *The Fashionable Theater*. Under the pretext of giving advice to singers, composers, enterpreneurs, librettists, stage designers, etc., it solemnly made fun of the Venetian protagonists of the music opera. Those protagonists were not indicated by their names, but with pseudonyms obtained by anagraming their names, so that the allusions were very transparent. Vivaldi appeared as "Mr. Aldiviva," and was satirized without mercy. A satirical drawing depicted him with the violin in his hand, with his priest hat in the head with angel wings (reference to the Sant'Angelo theater with which Vivaldi had frequent relationships) and with a foot raised in the act of imperiously scanning the tempo (it was a gesture that Vivaldi used to do and express effectively the position of power that he had as orchestra conductor and theater enterpreneur). The volume was anonymous, but it was then known that it had been written by Benedetto Marcello, an intelligent Venetian composer.

Among the singers, the one who worked for Vivaldi for a long time was Anna Giraud (surname Italianized in Girò), of French origin. Her voice was not so great. However, she knew how to move well on the scene, and her good skills as actress compensated for her limits as a singer.

Vivaldi's familiarity with Girò (and his sister, who worked for him as an housekeeper) aroused gossips and ostracisms, to which, however, he reacted lively, claiming the absolute correctness of his relationship with the two sisters.

The theater also allowed Vivaldi to meet in 1735 with a great contemporary, Carlo Goldoni, who was born in 1707 and was at the beginning of his career as a playwright. Goldoni, on an autobiographical page, sketched a vivid description of their encounter.

Vivaldi, impressed by the theatrical success that had had a Goldoni's comedy, asked him to help him transform the drama of Apostle Zeno, Griselda, into a music work. The encounter between them is amusing. Vivaldi is saying the breviary; on Goldoni's arrival he pauses and explains what he needs. Goldoni asks for paper, pen and inkwell to get to work right away and prove to him that he understood. Vivaldi remains a little surprised at such speed and shows some doubts about the results of such improvisation. Goldoni gets irritated, but Vivaldi tells him: "Don't be angry; you can sit at the table; here is paper, inkwell and booklet; make you comfortable". As Goldoni sets off to work, he resume the brewery's prayer. When Goldoni finished, he handed the sheet to Vivaldi; the latter sits down and reads carefully, holding the paper in the left hand and the breviary in the right hand.

"When he finishes with reading," writes Goldoni, "he casts the breviary aside, stands up, embraces me, runs to the door, calls Mrs. Annina (Girò) and her sister Paolina; he reads my work to them with a loud voice, then shouts: "He did it here, here he did it" and again he embraces me and says that I'm good, that I became his Dear, his Poet, his Confident, and he never abandoned me".

From this page arises the image of a courteous man, ready to acknowledge the dignity of others, easy to enthusiasm, communicative, friendly. Especially the enthusiasm is remarkable. It comes to mind the enthusiasm that animated the musician when he invented a new melody, when he discovered a new combination of instrumental timbres, when the orchestra of the "pute" performed to perfection one of his freshly composed and yet fresh ink concert.

Vivaldi wrote many plays: *Tito Manlio, Farnace, Ottone in villa, L'incoronazione di Dario, Griselda, Armida al campo d'Egitto,*

L'Olimpiade, etc. But his fame as a musician doesn't come from them: also because theater work was, at that time, limited by fixed and conventional schemes that mortified the inspiration. Vivaldi's theater had great success at that time, but today Vivaldi is remembered not for that music.

Much better known, and more valuable, are his compositions of sacred music: a genre that Vivaldi practiced with some assiduity and for which he left valuable pages: the *Stabat Mater*, two *Gloria*, a *Magnificat*, the *Beatus vir*, the *Te Deum* and others, as well as the oratorio *Juditha triumphans* devoted to the biblical heroine.

I would suggest listening to the first and second passage of *Gloria* RV 589. In the first (*Gloria in excelsis Deo*) we find all the vivacity and instrumental richness of Vivaldi; in the second (*Et pax in terra hominibus bonae voluntatis*), a peaceful and fascinating meditation on peace.

Let's not forget, then, the first piece of the *Stabat Mater* RV 621. As known, the *Stabat Mater* is an ancient Latin sequence (written by Jacopone da Todi, one of the last Latin-speaking poets and one of the first in Italian language), meditating on the pain of the Madonna at the foot of the cross: it is a great poem on the maternal pain.

The first verse says: Stabat Mater dolorosa / juxta crucem lacrimosa / dum pendebat filius... («The Mother was grieved, weeping, by the cross from which the Son was hanging...»). Let's listen to how Vivaldi expresses the mother's torment, immobile, almost petrified in his pain, helpless in the face of the unspeakable suffering of the Son, reduced by his executioners to a "thing" hanging from the wood of the cross. Vivaldi assigns the singing to the deep and dark voice of a contralto female voice, full of intense and engaging vibrations. That voice spreads its weeping supported and accompanied by waves of strings and continuo bass accords: sore and stormy waves, expressing immense pity and effectively point out the storm that shakes the soul of the Mother.

Finally, it would be worth listening to the first piece of the Vivaldi's *Te Deum* whose introduction, dominated by trumpets, reminds us of the splendor of the Sacrae Symphoniae conceived by Giovanni Gabrieli for the wonderful acoustics of the basilica of San Marco.

But, as we have seen, above all it's in the instrumental music that Vivaldi's art has touched its highest vertices.

SOME GREAT SUCCESSES.
THEN... VANISHED INTO THIN AIR

Years of great success follow: in Mantua, where he is invited by the governor Prince of Assia and where he remains for three years; in Milan, where he presents a pastoral drama (*La Silvia*) and an oratorio about the Magi; in Rome, where Pope Benedict XIII invited him to listen to some of his compositions; back to Venice, then to Vienna and Prague.

During these pilgrimages, as I have already mentioned, he encounters Emperor Charles VI, who will invite him to move to Vienna. Vivaldi will accept the invitation, also because the tastes of the Italian public are changing (for example, the Neapolitan work is affirming in all Italian theaters and is obscuring the "theatrical triumphs" of Vivaldi's music).

On March 21st 1740, Vivaldi directed Pietà a concert in honor of prince Federico Cristiano of Poland. It is a memorable concert for the pomp of the frame and for the splendor of the Vivaldi's music that is performed there. No one imagines that this is the last concert of Vivaldi in his Venice.

In the following September, Vivaldi left Venice after having received a closeout from the Pietà Hospital, where he had worked for his entire life. The departure to Vienna takes place in a climate of extreme discretion, almost secretly.

However, in Vienna he did not have the fortune he deserved: the emperor who had invited him died suddenly, and controversies concerning succession aroused. In that political situation of Austria, Vivaldi found himself being marginalized, almost ignored.

On the other hand, in Venice they were no longer talking about him, and his music was forgotten. In the archives of the Republic of Venice an anonymous recorder will write later: "The abbot Antonio Vivaldi, a very fine violinist, known as the Red Priest, an esteemed composer of concerts, earned 50.000 ducats in his days, but for disproportionate prodigality he died miserable Vienna".

Beyond this poor news, nothing else. As I said, in Venice Vivaldi was forgotten. What was his life in Vienna? When and how did he die?

Until eighty years ago we did not know anything about that. In 1938, the fog of the mystery began to dwindle: a researcher (Rodolfo Gallo) found in the archives of the church of St. Stephen in Vienna (which is the Cathedral of the Austrian capital) the act of death of Vivaldi, thanks to which we have a bit of light on some elements of that mysterious story.

The act of death is dated July 28th 1741 and it simply says: "July 28th 1741. The very reverend Mr. Antonio Vivaldi, priest, at Satler's house, near the Carinthia gate in the hospital cemetery. A small bells sound". Later it says that he died of internal inflammation, that he was sixty years old and that for the funeral the cost note had been 19,45 florins.

According to the date of that act, it would appear that Vivaldi lived in Vienna for only ten months. But nothing comes out about the way he lived in those months and about the music he possibly composed during them.

In all likelihood, the house where Vivaldi died, demolished in 1858, stood where today the building exists marked with numbers 47-49 of the Vienna Kärntnerstrasse, not far from the St. Stephen's Cathedral.

Let's now listen to the *Concert in tromba marina* P. 16. It is called that way because some violins imitate the "trombe marine" (medieval instruments with an arc, with a triangular or trapezoidal chassis, which produced a sound similar to a tiny trumpet voice: the "tromba marina" in fact). Together with the violins in tromba marina, some mandolins and ancient instruments such as theorbos and "salmò" play, offering inedited and beautiful sounds.

VIVALDI TODAY

The mysterious disappearance of Vivaldi accompanied - as I said - the oblivion of his music. They began to rediscover it in the nineteenth century, in parallel with the rediscovery of Bach's music.

Today, Vivaldi shines in the firmament of the great composers as one of the most astonishing stars: so that Claude Baignères has been able to speak, tastily, of "life, death and resurrection of Vivaldi".

His music attracts huge crowds, especially juvenile. The secret of this "catch" on today's public is in the style I mentioned: a style full of rhythms and colors. Massimo Mila - an unforgettable musicologist

29

from Turin, whom I was lucky to know personally - spoke of "animal health of the Vivaldi's rhythm that flows smoothly like the blood in the veins of a well-disposed organism"; and indeed that strong rhythm has a sort of vitality that drags and enthuses.

But the musical invention does not stop there: knowingly alternates Allegri and Adagi, offering a rich array of emotions and passing from the fiery and overwhelming impulse to the meditative and intimist abandonment. Orchestration is no longer - as it was in previous composers - a mere technical support to the melody, but becomes an expressive medium that uses an "instrumental grammar", resulting from a careful and passionate experimentation.

In this way, Vivaldi, who provided with his music moments of joy to the girls of the Hospital of Pietà, being without a family and saddened by the rigid and anonymous discipline of college life, comes back to give the young people of today (as well as the elderly) the joy of listening to a music full of brio, of liveliness, of warm lyricism: in a word, of young music that seems to have come out of the mind of a composer close to the soul of the contemporary man.

LISTENING GUIDE TO A MASTERPIECE:
CONCERTS OF THE FOUR SEASONS

It is probably the most famous work of Vivaldi. These are four concerts that are part of the collection *Il Cimento dell'Armonia e dell'Invenzione* (op. 8), including twelve concerts. The four seasons concerts are linked to each other by a unitary design, which makes it an autonomous masterpiece, of a compact unity. Each of the concerts is dedicated to a season, from which it takes the title. We have thus *Spring* (op. 8, n. 1, P. 241), *Summer* (op. 8, n. 2, P. 336), *Autumn* (op. 8, n. 3, P. 257), *Winter* (op. 8, n. 4, P. 442).

The four concerts are inspired, as their titles indicate, to the nature and the coming of the seasons. One might think that it is simply descriptive music, which merely transcribes the various voices of nature (noises of natural phenomena, voices of animals, etc.). Instead, it is not a music that "mimics" nature, but a music that, inspired by nature, creates wonderful musical architectures that have their own sense and their own artistic autonomy, irrespective of their reference to nature. In essence, the nature inspiration does not indulge in mere description, but it is inspired by it to elevate itself to authentic poetry and to soar to the highest music. This, however, does not exclude Vivaldi's ability to exploit the imitative abilities of the instruments, and especially of the violin, to obtain special effects (from the dog's barking to the song of the birds, from the murmur of the waters to the rumble of thunders), which will then find extensive use in the later violinistic literature (think about Paganini, expecially).

The four concerts are illustrated by four sonnets of the time. The origin of the sonnets is - as is the case with many of Vivaldi's life events - mysterious. We don't know who the author is. We don't known if they have been composed before the concerts (and therefore may have been the inspiration) or after (and thus constitute a literary commentary). The second hypothesis is more likely, and there are also those who think that Vivaldi may have written the sonnets himself. It is only known that they appeared in the first press edition of the concerts, published in Amsterdam.

They are sonnets of mediocre literary value. They are useful, however, to provide a listening guide for those who come for the first time to this Vivaldi work.

I will transcribe each of the sonnets, accompanied by some indication about the concert.

Spring

Springtime is upon us.
The birds celebrate her return with festive song,
and murmuring streams are softly caressed by the breezes.

Thunderstorms, those heralds of Spring, roar,
casting their dark mantle over heaven,
Then they die away to silence,
and the birds take up their charming songs once more.

On the flower-strewn meadow,
with leafy branches rustling overhead,
the goat-herd sleeps, his faithful dog beside him.

Led by the festive sound of rustic bagpipes,

nymphs and shepherds lightly dance beneath
the brilliant canopy of spring.

Poetry	Music
First verse: Joy and playfulness of nature.	*First movement:* Allegro.
Second verse: Threat for a thunderstorm. Then the threat dissolves.	Stormy atmosphere. Then, back to cheerfulness.
Third verse: Rest of the nature.	*Second movement:* Largo.
Fourth verse: Shepherd's zampoo and pastoral dance.	*Third movement:* Allegro.

The beginning of the first movement is extremely famous: a whippy, vigorous *Allegro* that evokes the festive awakening of nature in spring. The orchestra is all a vibration of voices, in which it is easy to distinguish the trill of the birds, the fresh murmur of the water, the swishing of the fronds to the spring breeze; the short parenthesis of a quick rainstorm silences those voices only for a moment, which soon resume their song. The second movement is a *Largo*, which evokes a pastoral scene: a pause of quiet and peace. The third movement is again an *Allegro*, who introduces a pastoral dance. It evokes the Arcadia, a literary movement that, in the 18th century, reacted to Baroque, being inspired by the world of Greek classicism and idealizing the pastoral environment as a model of simplicity and love for nature.

Summer

Beneath the blazing sun's relentless heat
men and flocks are sweltering, pines are scorched.
We hear the cuckoo's voice;
then sweet songs of the turtle dove and finch are heard.

Soft breezes stir the air...
but threatening north wind sweeps them suddenly aside.
The shepherd trembles, fearful of violent storm
and what may lie ahead.

His limbs are now awakened from their repose
by fear of lightning's flash and thunder's roar,
as gnats and flies buzz furiously around.

Alas, his worst fears were justified,
as the heavens roar and great hailstones beat down
upon the proudly standing corn.

Poetry	Music
First verse:	*First movement:*
Effects of the heatwave.	Slow music, which expresses
Suffering and prostration.	exhaustion.
Second verse:	Singing of a bird.
The breeze relieves the heat.	The wind relieves the heat.
	But a strong thunderstorm
	threatens.
Third verse:	*Second movement:*
Early signs of a thunderstorm.	Music describes the beginning
	of thunderstorm.
Fourth verse:	*Third movement:*
The storm shakes.	Music describes the damage the
	thunderstorm produces.

In the great summer heat the whole nature is dozed; only the song of some birds breaks the heavy silence, dominated by the sultriness and the prostration. A hurricane is peeking out at the horizon, which is obscured and becomes dark and threatening. Summer is a season of strong colors, of opposing excesses. In front of the threat (which is quite different from the announcement of a short, refreshing thunderstorm), the shepherd is taken by anguish. Then the hurricane explodes: it is all music, with a prodigious richness of rhythms that characterizes the third concert movement (a *Presto*).

Autumn

The peasant celebrates with song and dance
the harvest safely gathered in.
The cup of Bacchus flows freely,
and many find their relief in deep slumber.

The singing and the dancing die away
as cooling breezes fan the pleasant air,
inviting all to sleep
without a care.

The hunters emerge at dawn, ready for the chase,
with horns and dogs and cries.
Their quarry flees while they give chase.
Terrified and wounded, the prey struggles on,
but, harried, dies.

Poetry	Music
First verse: Joy of the harvest, followed by sleeping.	*First movement:* Joyful music, followed by a general sleep favored by good wine.
Second verse: Sleep and silence, supported by the sweet autumn climate.	*Second movement:* Slow and sweet music that accompanies sleep.
Third verse: Autumn is also a hunting season. Hunters chase the game, trap it in a circle and kill it.	*Third movement:* Music describes the pursuit of the game, the excitement of hunters, the death of the prey.

The first movement celebrates the joy of harvest: great animation in the farmyards; the music intonates a happy festive march, and then pierced it into whims of cheerfulness. Wine drives to singing and dancing.

The second movement is an *Adagio*. It opens with arpeggios of the harpsichord, on which a melody of the arches leans: the silvery tone of the harpsichord, mixed with the soft voice of the arches, creates a feeling of mystery, a veiled atmosphere.

The sonnet tells about sleep, the relaxation that takes on the excited rhythm of the party. But music says a lot more. It suggests the sweet, melting melancholy of Autumn: an intimate season, made of delicate colors, of half-autumn colors; veiled by the melancholy of the fallen leaves, the days shrinking, the cold approaching. A melancholy that has its secret serenity: the joy of intimacy, friendship, cheerful conversation. A calm and intimate joy, made palpable by the fact that strings instruments play with mutes.

Third movement, hunting. It begins with a march in which the echo of hunting horns is heard: a fair and slightly humorous march, in front of these hunters who, numerous, well armed and well protected by dogs, bravely go against a poor beast whose inevitable destiny will be to be overwhelmed. Then the music urges, as in a pursuit stroking the prey. A solo violin seems to express the last wriggles of the prey, his solitude, his death destiny. Finally, the march resumes, greets the triumph of the hunters and closes the piece.

Winter

Shivering, frozen mid the frosty snow in biting, stinging winds;
running to and fro to stamp one's icy feet,
teeth chattering in the bitter chill.

To rest contentedly beside the hearth,
while those outside are drenched by pouring rain.
We tread the icy path slowly and cautiously,
for fear of tripping and falling.

Then turn abruptly, slip, crash on the ground
and, rising, hasten on across the ice lest it cracks up.

We feel the chill north winds coarse through the home
despite the locked and bolted doors…
this is winter, which nonetheless brings its own delights.

Poetry	Music

First verse: The verses describe the nature of winter, the frosty frost, the cold that paralyces travelers.	*First movement:* The music expresses very effectively the discomfort produced by cold and ice.
Second verse: The joy of staying warm while out it is raining. But there are also those who have to walk on the ice and be careful not to fall.	*Second movement:* Sweet music that evokes the joy of staying warm, in the intimacy of your own home.
Third verse: There are also those who enjoy skating.	*Third movement:* Very lively music that expresses the charm of winter sports.
Fourth verse: Even the winds of the winter have their poetry.	*Fourth movement:* So winter can also be a source of joy.

An *Allegro* of extraordinary suggestion, full of dissonances, evokes the rigors of cold. The violin makes shivering evolutions. Then it is a race of the various instruments, with strong accelerations, with sudden slowdowns, with the enrichment of biting dissonances. The second movement is dominated by a warm melody sung by the violin and accompanied by the pinch of the other strings: it evokes the intimacy of the house, the warmth of the heated fireplace, and the lovable conversation, while out there are only wind and rain (the latter described with the insistent and regular pinch). A masterful page for the extended musicality, for the richness of suggestions.

The third movement is a very lively *Allegro*. Winter is depicted in a humorous, affectionate, joyful dimension. There are those who slip on the ice and are likely to fall; but there are also those who skate with elegance. The music alternates the softness of the wise lope of the skater, the biting stiffness of the cold, the fear of those who walk concentrated on where their feet are and totally absorbed by the concern not to slip to the ground. It's a wonderful musical game, where moments of concentration alternate to moments of unleashing. The latter are the final ones, characterized by real orchestral acrobatics: all in a climate that can be said to be joyful and that returns one of its real dimensions to winter. Also winter is life, indeed.

GETTING TO KNOW VIVALDI

The traditional numbering of Vivaldi's works is very incomplete. According to it, the collection of concerts named *Il Cimento dell'Armonia e dell'Invenzione* is indicated as op. 8; the collection named *L'Estro armonico* is numbered as op. 3, etc.

The most recent cataloguing are by the Italians Mario Rinaldi (1945) and Antonio Fanna (1968), by the Frech Marc Pincherle (1948) and by the Danish Peter Ryom (1973). These catalogues are commonly indicated with the letters R (Rinaldi), F (Fanna), P (Pincherle), RV (Ryom-Verzeichnis = Ryom Catalog).

The most popular catalogs are Pincherle and Ryom. The Fanna is a less easily quoted catalog because it involves the use of Roman numerals next to Arabic numerals (for example: F X, n. 2; F VI, n. 4).

I preferred to use Pincherle's catalog (P followed by an Arabic number) or the Ryom catalog (RV followed by an Arabic number).

Two are the books on which I deepened my initial knowledge of Vivaldi: Mario Rinaldi, *Antonio Vivaldi*, Milano 1943, a very large and detailed monograph; Michelangelo Abbado, *Antonio Vivaldi*, Arione, Turin 1942, a quick and essential profile.

Other more recent books are: Remo Giazotto, *Antonio Vivaldi*, Nuova Accademia, Milano 1965; Michael Talbot, *Vivaldi* (translation by Comba), ERI, Torino 1978; Id., *Vivaldi. Fonti e letteratura critica*, Olschki, Firenze 1991; Walter Kolneder, *Vivaldi*, Rusconi, Milano 1981; Remo Giazotto, *Invito all'ascolto di Vivaldi*, Mursia, Milano 1984; Cesare Fertonani, *Antonio Vivaldi. La simbologia musicale nei concerti a programma*, Studio Tesi, Pordenone 1992; Id., *La musica strumentale di Antonio Vivaldi*, Olschki, Firenze 1998; Jean-François Labie, *Vivaldi, il prete rosso*, Electa/Gallimard, Parigi 1996; Paul Everett, *Vivaldi: Le quattro stagioni e gli altri concerti dell'op. VIII*, Marsilio, Venezia 2000; Antonio Fanna e Michael Talbot, *Vivaldi vero e falso: problemi di attribuzione*, Olschki, Firenze 1992; Francesco Degrada, *Vivaldi veneziano europeo*, Olschki, Firenze 1980; Hermann Haller, *Vivaldi: cronologia della vita e dell'opera*,

Olschki, Firenze 1991; Federico Maria Sardelli, *La musica per flauto di Vivaldi*, Olschki, Firenze 2001; Mario Rinaldi, *Il teatro musicale di Vivaldi*, Olschki, Firenze 1979; Andrew Woolley, *Uno sconosciuto concerto (detto «Il gran Mogol») per flauto di Vivaldi, scoperto in Scozia*, in *Studi vivaldiani*, Fondazione Cini, Venezia 2010, pages 3-38; Pier Giuseppe Gillio, *L'attività musicale negli Ospedali di Venezia nel Settecento*, Olschki, Firenze 2006.

About Vivaldi I also indicate the short but fraught paper by Cesare Fertonani, *Orchestre e stili orchestrali*, included in the *Enciclopedia della Musica*, edited by Jean-Jacques Nattiez, Einaudi, Torino 2004, vol. IV, pages 498-513; and also Rodolfo Venditti, *Musica e teologia nei «Magnificat» di Vivaldi e di Bach*, in *Archivio teologico torinese*, Elledicì, Torino 2006, pages 191-207.

About the specific topics of Vivaldi's family and death can be seen: Rodolfo Gallo, *Antonio Vivaldi, il Prete Rosso: la famiglia, la morte*, in *Ateneo Veneto*, dec. 1938.

An interesting news about Vivaldi's compositions is this: in Turin, in the National Library, there are preserved Vivaldi's manuscripts relating to a large number of concerts (296) and several other instrumental pages as well as 60 pages of religious or sacred music (including the beautiful *Stabat Mater*), various singing and serenades and 20 theatre plays. The history of such manuscripts is very complex; for those who want specific instructions, they can start from a paper by Leonardo Osella, published on TorinoSette (included in "La Stampa", Turin newspaper) on February 10th 2006, titled *Lo scrigno di Vivaldi*.

JOHANN SEBASTIAN BACH
(1685-1750)

An ocean of music.
The tireless work of a non-violence cantor

Elias Gottlob Haussmann, *Johann Sebastian Bach at the age of 61*,
1746, William H. Scheide's private collection, Princeton, New Jersey, USA.

Johann Sebastian Bach was born on March 21st 1685 in Eisenach, Thuringia, a region of eastern Germany. His is a very large and ancient family: a real "dynasty" of musicians, joining Veit Bach, a miller and guitar player, who came to Germany from Hungary in the sixteenth century. A family full of uncles, granduncles and cousins, scattered throughout Germany; and also full in brothers, because Johann Sebastian is the last of eight brothers, three of whom are musicians.

The German word "bach" means "stream". It has been said, tastefully, that the Bachs were not a stream, but a vast and powerful river that crossed the centuries.

For the young Johann Sebastian that great river was providential. In fact, when he was nine he missed his mother, and at ten, his father. But he was not alone and lost: the immense family was a protective net for him that prevented him from falling into solitude. He was welcomed by his brother Johann Cristoph, who was married and lived in a not far city, Ohrdruf, where he was an organist. In his brother, the boy found not only the family welcome he needed, but also a careful and thoughtful music teacher, concerned about giving him gradual and progressive lessons. However, the boy, heavily inclined to music, ran ahead of the teacher's tuition; and since his brother had forbidden him to approach earlier and more difficult music, Johann Sebastian stood up by night, reached the closet that contained those music, collected in a "forbidden notebook," passing his small hand through the the grid of the door, rolled up the notebook, pulling it out, and copying the music sheets using the moonlight.

At the age of fifteen Johann Sebastian is sent to college in Lüneburg, where he becomes a choralist and starts studying the violin. He has opportunities to travel to Hamburg and Celle, to have contacts with the great organist Reinken, to learn French music, to assimilate the influences of the German organ school of the North and of the South. He becomes a good organist and also a good organar, that is, an expert in the construction and the mechanics of the organ and, hence, an organ tester: a very sought-after and not easy work, considering the complexity of an organ of those times, made up of hand-operated mantits, pipes, pedals, registers, multiple keyboards. Note that the organ has been defined as the most complex machine of the pre-industrial age.

ORGANAR AND ORGANIST AT THE AGE OF EIGHTEEN

And it's just the organar activity that gives the young Bach the first stable job. His fame as expert in this area drives the municipality of Arnstadt, a town in Thuringia, to entrust to him the testing of the new organ of the Neue Kirche, the new church built on the ruins of a former church destroyed in a fire.

And as the testing involves not only the technical check of the good functioning of the organ's mechanisms, but also the execution of some pieces by the tester, the triumphant execution of Bach on the new organ convinces the city to offer him the organist position in the same rebuilt church. Bach accepts with comprehensible pride and enthusiasm. It's 1703, and the boy is eighteen.

Arnstadt is a city where a lot of music is made, both sacred and profane. Bach has the opportunity to engage not only as a performer, but also as a composer. He writes organ music; to this period a beautiful piece belongs, which has become justly famous: the *Toccata e fuga* in D minor BWV 565. He also writes profane music. At that time, the great Bach family celebrates an important event, which gives Johann Sebastian the opportunity to write a composition for the harpsichord: his brother Johann Jacob was named oboe player at the court orchestra of the king of Sweden. On the occasion of the departure of Johann Jacob, all the Bachs in the neighboring regions come to Arnstadt for one of those nice family meetings that the Bach periodically were used to do, by strengthening their affection and solidarity links. Johann Sebastian celebrates his brother by composing for him the *Capriccio on the departure of a beloved brother.*

We can now immediately approach Bach's art by listening to *Toccata e fuga* in D minor BWV 565, one of the most famous Bach's organ pieces: the solemn majesty of *Toccata* follows the admirable construction of the *fuga*, in which the various voices run and recall each other through reciprocal engagements that give rise to a strong musical architecture.

Then let's listen to some passages of the *Capriccio on the departure of a beloved brother* BWV 992. The composition opens with an *Arioso* that expresses

41

the invitation of friends not to leave, the risks of going to a foreign country; an *Adagiosissimo* follows, expressing the lament of friends, who resign themselves to take leave from the departing guy; there is then an *Allegro poco* that evokes the recall of the driver of the coach that is coming and on which the departing guy will have to get on; finally, a *fuga* accompanies the departure of the beloved brother.

A RESTLESS YOUTH

Bach's relation with the Arnstadt municipality soon failed due to some incidents. Apart from the criticisms made to his way of playing, judged quite new, extravagant and complicated, there are some behaviors of his that fellow citizens don't like.

First of all, the fact that he let his cousin Maria Barbara, to whom he has a strong sympathy, to come up to the organ and chorus, a place forbidden by women.

Then, a quarrel with a certain Geyersbach. During some practice with the orchestra and chorus, Bach, who is just over twenty, severely reproves some members of the ensemble, unruly and, perhaps, incapable of having to submit to a director younger than them. He especially reproves a bassoon player (Geyersbach, in fact) and addresses the Zippelfagottist epithet ("small-time bassoon player"). The bassoon player does not forget the insult and revenges himself: one evening, backed by friends, assaults Bach on the street with a cudgel; Bach pulls out the sword and follows a brawl, resulting in a city scandal and a judicial inquiry.

Third fact: Bach asks for permission to go to Lübeck to hear Buxtehude, a great organist who plays in the beautiful Marienkirche of that northern city, a few hundred kilometers from Arnstadt. He is granted a four-week leave; he leaves, making the long journey on foot; he listens to Buxtehude several times, and his stay away from Arnstadt extends to four months. It's too much. At Arnstadt the big fault is not forgiven and he is fired. It's 1707.

MATRIMONIAL PROBLEMS

In truth, Bach had been tempted to come to Buxtehude (who was about to retirement) as the organist of the Marienkirche in Lübeck. But he had given up because one of the clauses set by the city for this succession required for the successor to marry the daughter of the outgoing organist: a daughter who was ten years older than Bach and, moreover, it seems that she was not at all attractive.

Apart from the oddity of this obligation, Bach was sentimentally tied to his cousin Maria Barbara, whom he would soon marry and build a happy family blessed by seven children.

Meanwhile, after his dismissal from the city of Arnstadt, Bach found another job in Mülhausen, a town where Pietism prevails, a current of Lutheranism based on the conception of a "church of the heart". Pietism devalued much the role of music in the sacred context. Bach feels uncomfortable, prevented in expressing himself completely. In Mülhausen he stays for a short period and he soon moves to Weimar.

Weimar is the city destined to become, in a few decades, a very important center of culture, to the point to earn the title of "German Athens". In those years it is still a very small town; but there sacred music is greatly appreciated and Bach can devote himself to a very intense organ production. Thus, he wrote many church cantatas and the Orgelbüchlein ("Little Organ Book"), a collection of 46 chorale preludes for organ.

Among the church cantatas there is the famous *Actus Tragicus*, composed in the months of Mülhausen. It is called that way because it was written for a funeral: but the naming is improper and cheating because, in fact, this cantata has nothing tragic. Composed on beautiful biblical texts, it is animated by a festive joy, which perfectly translates the serene vision of death that the Christian faith offers.

In Weimar, then, Bach makes a valuable acquaintance: he meets organist Walther, who is passionate about Italian music and let him know the music of Italian composers. Bach learns avidly those music and transcribes for execution with organ or harpsichord many orchestral compositions by Corelli, Vivaldi, Albinoni, discovering the treasures of Italian instrumental music. In Weimar, on the other hand, he does not only perform organist tasks: he is also a member of the ducal orchestra, playing violin and viola.

Bach and Vivaldi were contemporary, yet they never met in person because of the shortage and slowness of the means of transport at that time (remember that they were traveling in horse-drawn carriages, so each journey was characterized by extreme slowness and countless hardships). The contemporaneity of two great genes whose encounter could have been fruitful but never happened, always strikes me and I regret it. I think that mankind has lost an extraordinary opportunity for spiritual growth and enrichment.

The choices for listening something of the Bachian production of this period are countless. We can listen to some cantatas, for example, the BWV 61 *Nur komm, der Heiden Heiland*, or some chorales from the *Orgelbüchlein* (for example, the Christmas chorales BWV 614 and 615), or Bach's transcript for organ (BWV 593) of the Vivaldi's concert op. 3 n. 8 from *L'Estro armonico*. Regarding transcripts, Bach transcribed several Vivaldi's concerts (already six just from *L'Estro armonico*: n. 3, 8, 9, 10, 11, 12). We could also listen to the transcription for four harpsichords that Bach made of the Vivaldi's concert op. 3 n. 10 (such Bachian transcript is marked with the catalog number BWV 1065).

THE HAPPY PERIOD IN KÖTHEN (1717-1723):
INSTRUMENTAL MUSIC TRIUMPH

Bach leaves Weimar on his own initiative and rather indignant. They refused to give him the prestigious job as a Kapellmeister ("Master of chapel"), preferring another mediocre musician. He resigns, conflicting with the duke, who feels affronted and condemns him to a month of prisonment (at that time the court musician is considered a servant, and his self-dismissal tastes as an intolerable offense to the master). But Bach does not feel intimidated. And he will not have reason to regret his decision because he finds a better work placement at Köthen, where they immediately offer the highly demanded role of Kapellmeister. It is 1717 and Bach is thirty-two years old.

At the court of the Principality of Köthen, a Calvinist city, they give no great importance to sacred music, but the chamber music, the orchestra and the harpsichord are much loved. Prince Leopold is a twenty-three-year-old man, intelligent and passionate about music. He studied in Berlin; he traveled to France, Italy, England; he plays various instruments. With Bach, he immediately establishes an excellent relationship of trust and admired worship. He takes Bach with him in various journeys, he estimates him, he enjoys his achievements and considers them as his own pride, he asks him for advice on purchasing instruments. One of those journeys in 1717 has Dresden as a destination: there Bach meets the great violinist Pisendel who has just come back from Italy where he met Vivaldi, took lessons from him, listened to the latest Vivaldi compositions, carrying the music sheets in Dresden. During another of these trips, Bach has the opportunity to know the Margrave of Brandenburg, who appreciates him very much and will invite him other times. Bach will write for him six concerts, which will be called *Brandenburg Concertos*. They are six masterpieces of instrumental music, in which the different instruments of the orchestra are used in various and original combinations, full of effects and colors.

It is worth to taste them.

The *first* concert is very wide and articulated: I especially point out the second movement, delicate and meditative, as well as the *Minuetto* that opens the fourth movement.

The *second* concert is dominated by the trumpet and is constructed according to the Vivaldi form of the *concerto grosso*, that is a dialogue between a "concertino" (group of four instruments: trumpet, flute, oboe, violin) and an "all" (composed of the above instruments plus two violins, viola, violone, cello, harpsichord): the first movement is mostly fascinating.

The *third* concert, which is for strings and harpsichord, is a "group" concert, that is a highly-fledged dialogue between three groups of instruments. The great orchestra conductor Furtwängler, while giving his orchestra the interpretative indications, said that this concert makes you think of the animated square of a small town on a festive day, when all the inhabitants are party dressed and talk and chat, in a dense, constant, animated and civil cackle. This is a lovely concert, consisting of two very fast movements, linked by a slow joint, consisting of only two chords.

The *fifth* concert is perhaps the most well known and performed. In the first movement the flute prevails. But the whole composition is dominated by the harpsichord, to which a final solo piece (the so-called cadence) is dedicated.

Of the *sixth* concert I point out the last movement, beautiful for the greatness it acquires, even with very simple music.

But the Köthen period is characterized not only by the Brandenburg Concertos. It is rich in various instrumental production. Earlier, musicologists thought that this time was for Bach a period of mortification, a kind of "golden cage", because in it he had not been able to properly practice his favorite sacred music. Today critique has changed: through research and studies, made public in a book by Piero Buscaroli, it pointed out that the period of Köthen was neither a "golden cage" nor a rest period during which Bach's art was silent, but it was a time of intense and volcanic production, during which Bach, while leaving aside his favorite sacred music, was able to perform with lively satisfaction a rich production activity of instrumental music, creating high-end masterpieces for orchestra, violin, cello and harpsichord.

It is enough to remember the *Orchestra Suites*, the *Concertos for violin and orchestra*, the *Sonatas and Partitas for solo violin*, the first book of *The well-tempered clavier*, the *Suites for cello solo*.

Here we are spoiled for choice. From the *Orchestra Suites* I would like to listen to the second one (BWV 1067: containing a delightful *Minuetto* and a whippy *Badinerie*) and the third one (BWV 1068: containing the famous *Aria*, then called "on the G string", and a delicious *Gavotta*).

From the *Concertos for violin* I would point out the BWV 1042, whose second movement (characterized by an intimate and meditative melody) documents how often Bach's profane work (i.e. not expressly religious work) is inspired by a profound religious sense (in fact this melody was used by the movie director Pasolini as the leading theme of the film *The Gospel According to Matthew*), and the BWV 1041, in which once again Bach demonstrates how to make a clever use of bass. Nor should the *Concerto for two violins and orchestra* BWV 1043 be neglected: I recommend listening to the second movement, extraordinary for the sweet dialogue between the two leading violins.

From the six *Sonatas and Partitas for solo violin* (BWV 1001-1006) written by Bach in this period of Köthen, I recommend listening to the second partita (BWV 1004), which contains the famous *Ciaccona* (*chaconne* is the French name of a dance): it's a tough piece, but even those who are not used to this kind of musical language will realize the prodigious polyphony that Bach can extract from the violin. Then listen to the third partita, the last part of which is a delicious *Gavotte en rondò*, in French gallant style.

Bach is able to extract also a prodigious polyphony from the cello in the six *Suites for cello solo* (BWV 1007-1012): the third suite is emblematic.

We can then approach the first book of *The well-tempered clavier*, a collection of "exercises" designed to train students to move smoothly between the various major and minor keys: through the great art of Bach, these "exercises" become authentic masterpieces of high musical poetry. Let's take the BWV 846 exercise as an example: we are in front of a delicate sequence of arpeggios that seems ready for a passionate melody laying over it; and in fact, a century and a half later, Gounod will take from it the inspiration to write his famous *Ave Maria*, which is naturally born from the delicate arpeggios of the Bach's "exercise".

TWO SEVERE BLOWS

But the happiness of Köthen lasts a few years. On July 17th 1720, going back to Köthen from a business trip to Karlsbad (Bohemia), lasting about two months following Prince Leopold, Bach found a tremendous surprise: during his absence, his wife Maria Barbara died; the slowness of the communications at that time did not allow him to have timely news; and his wife's body was buried on July 7th 1720 without Bach giving her the last greetings.

It's a really severe blow. Maria Barbara was a good wife, and the musician is deprived of the beloved consort, and at the same time with a load of four children to look after (three others died very young).

Not only. Shortly afterward, Prince Leopoldo marries the princess Federica Enrichetta of Anhalt-Bernburg, a woman not loving music (Bach will define her with an *ad hoc* contrieved, extremely expressive adjective, "pricipessa amusa," that is a princess absolutely missing musical sensitivity). The woman exercises her negative influence on the husband on the musical stuff: the prince begins to abandon his musical interests, and for Bach this causes a great suffering. It's a second severe blow: Köthen's "happiness" is over, and Bach thinks about another placement.

In Leipzig, the job position of Kantor has become vacating at the Thomasschule, an orchestral and choir school that exists at the church of St. Thomas, with an ancient and prestigious tradition. Bach competes in that place, although for him, Kapellmeister, becoming Kantor is a sort of demotion. But life in Köthen does not attract him anymore; and on the other hand Leipzig offers prospects for university studies for the growing children. He wins the competition and moves to Leipzig. It is 1723.

FROM «STREAM» TO «OCEAN»

In the meantime, he also solved her serious family problems, by getting married again and thus giving a new maternal presence to his children. The new wife is Anna Magdalena Wilken: she is a sweet and intelligent woman who actively exercises singing, and hence deals with music; she was born in Thuringia, in the town of Zeitz, she belongs to a family whose members are almost all music professionals. Bach heard her singing at a concert in Weissenfels and proposed her to enter the choir of the Köthen court. Estimation will result in sympathy and then in a marriage proposal, which Anna Magdalena will accept. She will be for Bach an ideal wife, a tireless and painstaking collaborator, especially in copying musical scores: an important activity at that time, when the press was still underdeveloped and very expensive, and there were no other means to reproduce sheets of music. The calligraphy of Anna Magdalena will become progressively similar to her husband's one, insomuch that it becomes difficult to distinguish music sheets copied by Bach from the ones copied by his wife.

Anna Magdalena will give her husband fourteen children (some of whom died at an early age): so Bach's offspring will rise to twenty-one children altogether. And with the children surviving the childhood diseases, the Bachs will have the joy of creating a joyful, lively, intensely musical family: a family that every night turned into a rich and articulated musical complex that offered praise to God singing the music composed by the father. Bach himself writes to a friend,with smiling pride: "All my children are born musicians; I can arrange, when I want, a concert both *vocaliter* and *instrumentaliter*; my wife, in particular, has a pleasant soprano voice...".

And for this nice tribe, Bach will also start composing educational works to provide a trace of learning and deepening for his children, his wife and later for the students: among these works shines the first book of *The well-tempered clavier*, which we have already had the opportunity to know, and the *Klavierbüchlein* (Little Piano Book).

Among the spouses, the intent will be perfect. Anna Magdalena will say, with a devotion that today sounds even overwhelming (as it seems to take away from her any space of autonomy and make her live only in a reflected light): "I have no other life than his one; I am a small river in an ocean". And here's the "stream" Bach has become even an "ocean." It is a very beautiful and appropriate image, because it expresses the idea of Bach's immense inner and artistic wealth and of its endless musical production.

It is for Anna Magdalena that Bach writes a collection of compositions for harpsichord, the *Klavierbüchlein*, I just mentioned. Certainly for her, good singer, leaving Köthen (where she was affirmed and esteemed) and moving to Leipzig, a predominantly commercial city, should have meant to give up (at least part of) her role as an artist: after all, in Leipzig, her role simply became "wife of the Kantor" and "family mother."

Amongst the Bach's sons, three are going to become musicians of a certain level: Wilhelm Friedemann (who will be called "the Bach of Halle"), Carl Philip Emanuel ("the Bach of Hamburg") and Johann Christian (the most famous, "the Bach of London", because he will move to England). The Bach's "dynasty", then, increases and widens, even if the children do not reach the artistic peaks of the father. But above all, the father's production broadens, who fervently returns to the sacred music and now also includes the oratorio, creating the *St. John Passion*.

In Bach's time, in the Lutheran area, it was widespread to meditate, on Holy Friday, on Jesus' passion and death, meeting together in church and reliving the Lord's suffering through music and singing. A tenor read, singing, the text of the Gospel, and each character (Jesus, Peter, Pilate, Judas, Pilate's wife, etc.) was played by a soloist while the choir gave voice to the crowd. The reading was commented on by various songs, some of them solo (soprano, alto, tenor, baritone and bass), others of choral nature. These songs expressed the churchgoers' participation in the story: they were prayers, invocations, acts of repentance for own sins, promise of conversion and fidelity to the Gospel. Bach shown up in Leipzig with the *St. John Passion* just composed, which was performed on March 26th 1723 (or, according to recent studies, the following year).

We can now "taste" the *St. John Passion* (Johannes-Passion) BWV 245. As we will say later about the *St. Matthew Passion*, it is divided into numbers, corresponding to the various pieces that make it up. It is sung in German, so it is advisable to have text with the Italian translation in front. An intensely dramatic part is the dialogue between Jesus and Pilate. That part begins with n. 21, a chorus in which it is said: "Our Redeemer, without sin, was captured in the night as a cowardly criminal," and, after the dramatic talk between Pilate and the crowd, ends with the phrase of Pilate: "What I wrote, I wrote" (*Was ich geschrieben habe, das habe ich geschrieben*) (n. 51).

Another piece that you should listen to is the one that develops in the n. 57 and 58 and focuses on the last sentence of Jesus: "Everything is accomplished" (*Es ist vollbracht*).

I would like to point out: at n. 23 the crowd crying (looks like a inhumane howl) who says: "If he was not a criminal we would not have brought him to you"; at n. 36 the violent chorus of the crowd "Crucify him!" (*Kreuzige!*); at n. 38 the stubborn sentence *Wir haben ein Gesetz* ("We have a law"), with which the crowd responds to Pilate; the n. 42 ("If you leave him free, you're not a Caesar's friend"); the n. 46 where the crowd cries out: "We have no other king but Caesar!"; the n. 48,

49

with the tune of a bass dialoguing with the choir ("Run, run! Where, where? At the Golgotha"); the n. 54, in which the soldiers toss for the Jesus' tunic (it is a polyphonic masterpiece dominating the sense of the game, in a singular contrast to Christ dying on the cross).

Antonino Drago, who is a profound savant of nonviolence, found in this *Passion* a limit of Bach. Where the evangelist describes the slap given to Jesus during the interrogation in front of Caifa and the firm, serene and stringent nonviolent response that Jesus gives to his aggressor, calling on rationality, Bach does not give musical significance to such an important episode and therefore he does not grasp the opportunity to think over the extraordinary lesson of nonviolence coming from the behavior of Christ.

I agree with Drago: although I believe that this limit, derived both from the Lutheran sensibility of that time (influenced by pietism and therefore more inclined to devotionalism than to theological-philosophical meditation) and from the youthful age of Bach (the *St. John Passion* is, notoriously, a youthful and therefore less mature work compared to the *St. Matthew Passion*), is then redeemed by later Bach's compositions.

A DIFFICULT JOB

At St. Thomas's School in Leipzig, Kantor had multiple tasks: to teach Latin language and music, to instruct choirs, to compose cantatas for every Sunday, to direct musical performances during religious functions, to take part in weddings and funerals by playing proper organ music, to deal with discipline in the college close to the school...

A heavy and difficult work, especially as the school was at that moment in a deplorable state after years of neglect and disorganization: the students were unruly, the hygiene was lacking, the school performance was very low, the reputation of the school very impoverized. In addition, Bach soon collided, due to various administrative matters, with the civil and religious authorities, as well as with the University. There were several controversies that embittered him, in which he had to struggle to assert what he believed to be his rights.

But beyond pains and difficulties, this kind of activity offers Bach the opportunity to go back to sacred music and organ compositions, and to live a very fertile period: years of impetus and enthusiasm, during which several beautiful church cantatas, many organ chorales, lots of didactic music, and finally the magnificent masterpieces of the *St. Matthew Passion* (BWV 244) and the *Mass in*

B minor (BWV 232) are born. That a Lutheran as Bach made up a Catholic Mass (that is, music for a rite that is specifically Catholic and which was the reason for division among Christians) is something that has always surprised me. But positively surprised: almost to mean that different visions of Christianity can legitimately coexist, overcoming historical hate and sad wars of religion, in the common effort to grasp the substance of the Gospel message and to implement it with fraternal fidelity to the word of Christ.

About the *St. Matthew Passion* I will spend a specific paragraph later.

Here we can listen to some pieces of cantatas. For example, the cantata *Geist und Seele* ("Spirit and soul", BWV 35), or the cantata *Du Hirte Israel, höre* ("You pastor of Israel, listen," BWV 104). Or a few passages of the cited *Mass in B minor* (for example, *Gloria* or *Credo*). Of the *Credo*, I point out the impetuous *Et resurrexit*, expressing with explosive exultation the joy that the disciples felt in finding their Master, after the drama of passion and death on the cross, alive and present amongst them.

This return to sacred music does not exclude, however, that Bach continues to cultivate instrumental music. For example, in 1726 he created the *Partita n. 1* (BWV 825) for harpsichord, which will then be followed by five other partitas. Here the word "partita" has nothing to do with departure for a trip or a sporting encounter: even if the verb "partire", derived from the Latin, produced words that designate events of that kind, it is here used in the original meaning of "dividing into parts", and hence of instrumental composition consisting of multiple movements.

From the *Partita n. 1* I point out especially the last movement, which is a gigue, of a super-delicacy. Listening to it means - in my opinion - to experience a superb masterpiece, animated by a delicate and gentle inventive, which makes it an authentic jewel of grace and elegance, even in the very short space of 1 minute and 19 seconds. It is pleasing - in my humble opinion - the interpretation that pianist Glenn Gould gave it in his recording.

SOMETHING BREAKS

In 1736 and 1737 two facts broke that prodigious creative momentum and induced Bach to fall back on himself.

The first is the sharp contrast with the new school director, Johann Heinrich Ernesti junior, whose illuministic and rationalistic vision is diametrically opposite to Bach's religious-Lutheran vision. For him, a believer and heir of an age where religious faith was seen and felt as an essential component of social life, music is, in its essence, *elevatio cordis ad Deum* ("elevation of the heart to God", that is a mean of prayer).

For Ernesti, on the other hand, the task of education is not to train the believer, but to form the scientist, the rational, positivist man; so maths and sciences are more important than music. The two visions collide when it comes to naming the Kantor helper: Bach would want a young man very capable in the music but insufficient in other subjects (his name is Krause); Ernesti wants one who is good at all subjects. This yields in a hard quarrel, which will end with a compromise and which will greatly hurt Bach's prestige.

While on the one hand we can not disagree with Bach's claim to having a young man best-talented in music rather than in other subjects, on the other hand we can not ignore the note of exasperated radicalization that put up the two visions. Today, after the path that believers and unbelievers have made towards pluralism, mutual respect, autonomy of science and art with respect to religious faith, it seems a rather futile and sterile contrast, in which Bach is the loser.

But Bach was son of his days and his religious vision couldn't ignore the dominant mentality at that time: a mentality in which was still missing the principle that beliefs of a believer can not be imposed on a not-believer. Behind the clash of conceptions, however, there were also stubborn and conflicting interpretations of the right to name the so-called *praefectus chori*, as well as a certain dislike of the Leipzig citizens towards the frequent absences of the Kantor, often called in other cities for concerts or organs tests.

The second fact is the incident related to Bach's relationship with his student Scheibe. The latter attends a competition in which Bach is part of the jury; but since in the competition also appears a much better candidate than Scheibe, Bach, with a perfect examiner objectivity, votes in favor of the best: a magnificent example of honesty that should make us think over the plague of recommendation and favoritism, very widespread nowadays.

Scheibe, who is obviously a man of quite a different level, does not forgive Bach that behavior, and subsequently become a music critic in Hamburg, revenges himself by publishing a heavy criticism of Bach's way of composing. For Bach is another serious blow. Moreover, the style that is now spreading is the gallant style, inspired by frivolity, looking for delight, exalting one's voice over the others. It is the exact opposite of Bach's art, who conceives music as a deeply digging, a construction of sound architectures targeted to convey a message, a *laudatio Dei et recreatio cordis* ("praise of God and heart recreation"), a counterpoint and search for interiority.

This "break" pushes Bach to close himself and interiorize his music more and more. His art tends to break away from every functional destination, from every practical use, and becomes abstract research of increasingly rich and complex musical geometries: abstract not in the sense that it is detached from life but in the sense that it is detached from utilitarian purposes, albeit high and noble (such as those of a cantata or a Passion). That way the latest Bachian masterpieces are born: *The Musical Offering*, the *Goldberg Variations*, the *Schübler Chorales*, the second book of *The well-tempered clavier*, *The Art of Fugue*.

These extreme fruits of Bachian art will feed the musicians of tomorrow: Beethoven, who, under the guidance of his master Neefe, will study *The well-tempered clavier*; Mozart, who, through van Swieten, fortunate owner of many Bachian manuscripts, will be largely in touch with Bach's art; Chopin, who will have as master Ziwny, great admirer of Bach...

We can now listen to one of the *Schübler Chorales* (these are six chorales so called by the name of the publisher who printed them): for example, the BWV 645 chorale, *Wachet auf, ruft uns die Stimme* ("Awake, the voice calls us"), a strong and suggestive prayer that invites to an intense commitment of the spirit.

«LADIES AND GENTLEMEN, THE ELDERLY BACH IS HERE!»

In 1747 Bach travels to Berlin: he goes to see a son who lives there and hosts him in his own home. King Frederick II of Prussia immediately learns the news of his arrival, interrupts a party, announces to everyone, with a loud voice: "Ladies and gentlemen, the elderly Bach is here!". He immediately sends a carriage to the master, who does not even have time to change clothes. Touched by the impatience of the king, Bach gets on the carriage in a travel suit, still dusty, and goes to the court.

The king goes to meet him, receives him with all the honors, asks for an opinion on his pianos, then prays to play and suggests a theme to improvise.

Bach suddenly makes stunning variations on the kingly theme (that is, on the theme pointed out by the king) and, returning to Leipzig, will write those variations, re-elaborate and enrich them; he will then send the score to the king, entitling it *Offrande musicale* (Musical offering).

Let's listen to the kingly theme, and to some of the variations of the *Offrande musicale* (BWV 1079). We are in the presence of the most arduous and mature Bach.

TURNIPS, CABBAGE AND SLEEPLESSNESS
GIVE OUT TO A MASTERPIECE

Another of Bach's latest works, composed in the shape of the theme with variations, is the one called *Goldberg Variations*.

Goldberg was a young pupil of Bach, a sixteen-year-old harpsichord player. He had had a strange adventure: he had been summoned to the court of Saxony by the Russian ambassador, who suffered from insomnia and neurasthenia, and needed the harpsichord player to help him, playing the harpsichord during the night.

It is unclear if the music should have the function of driving the patient to sleep or only to calm his nerves and help him to hang out: perhaps there may be a curious example of music therapy here. But today there are those who question the historicity of this strange story: Alberto Basso, one of the most important experts about Bach, is inclined to relegate it to legend. At any rate it's a fact that Goldberg, after consuming all his harpsichord repertoire, turned to Bach inviting him to compose variations on a theme. Bach accepted and gave birth to an authentic masterpiece.

The inspiration of some variations is derived from the theme of popular songs, one of which reads as follows: "Cabbage and turnips have driven me away; if my mother had cooked some meat, I would have stayed longer". From this humble folk material, Bach was able to come to the highest artistic levels, creating the work under the name of *Goldberg Variations* BWV 988.

We can have a taste of the *Goldberg Variations*: the initial theme and some of the thirty variations - the one about "turnips and cabbage" is the last one. The *incipit* of the composition is unmistakable for its fascinating beauty: a calm and silken theme, simple at a first glance, but indeed endowed of a complexity from which an astonishing kaleidoscope of variations will arise.

«I COME TO YOUR THRONE, O LORD»

«Here is the elderly Bach», said the king. In truth, at that time Bach was sixty-two years old: by the meter with which today we measure old age, one could not say old, even though he had gone to the third age.

But at that time the average length of human life was much shorter than it is today: a quick turnaround even among musicians would remind us that Pergolesi died at twenty-six, Mozart at thirty-five, Schubert at thirty-one, Chopin at thirty-eight, Mendelssohn at thirty-eight, Weber at forty, Beethoven at fifty-seven. So, those who were sixty years old were considered old.

Bach's old age is afflicted by a gradual loss of sight. This is likely to have been influenced by the tremendous effort of thousands of hours spent reading and writing music at the candlelight.

Bach was visited and treated by an English surgeon, who was temporarily in Leipzig: Taylor. He was a famous surgeon, but at that time the medicine was extremely primitive, and one can easily imagine what it was a surgical work on eyes.

Bach's health worsened quickly. He died on the evening of July 28th 1750, at sixty-five, after having strangely recovered his sight for a few hours.

His last choral, which he was dictating to his son-in-law Altnikol, is inspired to a prayer that begins like this: "I come to your throne, o Lord". It is a significant coincidence. Bach had lived with deep faith in the presence of God, in his lordship, in his paternity. He had conceived and lived the music as *praeludium vitae aeternae*. He had frequently written on his musical scores the motto "Soli Deo gloria" ("Glory to God only") or the invocation "Iesu juva" ("Jesus, help me"). He had worked with honesty and righteousness, like a tireless craftsman of music, without big personal ambitions; he had adored with tenderness and fidelity the two wives who, in the history of his life, had been at his side; he had spent time and energy with joy for his children, a happy tribe that every morning gathered around her father to start the day singing praises to the Lord. He had had its rage and anger, signs of a temper somewhat shady and unfriendly, but rich in professional dignity. He had taken good care of his interests, often in conflict with his employers to protect his rights at times when the worker had little protection.

He had had also difficulties and frustrations: the premature death of his parents, the sudden death of his first wife, the death of several children, a severely handicapped child, blindness, moments of bitterness, misunderstandings, and economic hardships. But he had been a serene, sober, honest, happy man, firmly anchored to his Christian faith.

Those words suited him perfectly. They went on to say: "My whole person is in your hand / Turn to me your benevolent face, and do not deny your grace. / Tell me that my end will be sweet / That at the awakening I will stand before you / To know you for all eternity / Amen. O God, give me your promise".

The latest Bachian masterpiece, *The Art of Fugue*, remained unfinished. To me it's always exciting to listen to Fugue 19, which at some point is broken, as was the life of the master, in the middle of a maturity that still could have given many fruits.

From *The Art of Fugue* BWV 1080, let's listen to Fugue 19, until its interruption.

LISTENING GUIDE TO A MASTERPIECE:
ST. MATTHEW PASSION (MATTHÄUS-PASSION)

St. Matthew Passion is a drama of extraordinary power. His subject is already exceptional: Christ, the son of God, the man for excellence, the embodiment of goodness and love, is betrayed, tortured, put on the cross like a lamb brought to the slaughter. Around him are intense passions: the hatred of the Pharisees who want to eliminate him for his brave denunciation of their hypocrisy; the interests of the politicians (Pilate, Herod) who pass the buck to each other about the issues created by his presence; the turmoil of the fickle crowd, which yesterday was cheering at him and today is shouting "*Crucifige*"; the cold calculation of Judas, who for his greed of money betrays his master, delivering him to his adversaries; the infinite and indomitable fear of the disciples; the Peter's regret... And, above everything, the clear calm of Jesus, his perfect self-control and matership of situations, even in the darkness and distress, his love for others even in times of most intense suffering, his dying with shining and conscious acceptance of the human condition, his way to offer to the Father his sacrifice for the salvation of everybody.

Bach's deep religiosity has vibrated intensely at all stages of the drama and has given to it a wonderful musical interpretation. Some pieces are a bit difficult for man today due to the type of language and some prolixity; but others are tight and intense, they "bring" the listener and go straight to the heart, they immediately find the way to an immediate understanding. Gino Roncaglia said that Bach "blends the Palestrina's sacred style and the dramatic Schütz's style with Vivaldi's instrumental style, giving the mark of his energetic, dynamic, airy personality to this fusion".

To facilitate the execution and listening of the monumental work, the various pieces are numbered in progressive order. The text is, of course, in German language, according to the translation that Luther did of the Bible. Music is thought to be in line with that German text, although it does not remain subordinate to the word, but has its own artistic autonomy: so, performing it in other languages would betray Bach's art as it would distort the relationship between word and music. It is therefore appropriate to have the German text with a comfortable translation facing: the recordings have such an indispensable accessory; and, in concerts, programs normally carry the original text with the translated version.

The *Passion* begins with a great chorus that immediately makes us join the spirit of drama: the women of Jerusalem cry because the lamb of God (*Lamm Gottes*), humble and patient, is brought to the cross to be killed. A chorus of boys overlaps and invokes: "Have mercy on us, Jesus" (*Erbarm'dich unser, o Jesu*) (n. 1). After this introduction the story of the evangelist begins, starting from the moment Jesus tells his disciples that Easter is imminent and that the

Son of Man will be delivered into the hands of his opponents to be crucified.

The evangelist's tale is a sung reading of the evangelical text: a "dry" recital, accompanied only by a few essential harpsichord accords. However, this recitation is not impersonal and aloof: it is an intensely expressive song because the narrator lives the story, and his song perfectly adheres, in its inflections, to the moods that is gradually revealing.

The voice of Jesus is a beautiful baritone voice (we hear it right now in n. 2; we can hear it in n. 8 and then in n. 15, and so on). It is a masculine, incisive voice, full of charm and mystery. It always comes with a background of strings (violins and cellos), which creates a kind of sound aura and clearly distinguishes it from the voice of any other character in the drama.

The n. 15 is intensely dramatic; Jesus says: "Some of you will betray me"; and that "will betray me" is expressed with vibrations of intense pain. Here is the chorus of the apostles who ask: "Lord, am I that one?" (Herr, bin ich's?): and the choral setting of the song also involves the listener, who feels being part of those for whom Jesus died. And involvement is immediately underlined by the next choral (n. 16), where the churchgoer directly enters the drama, saying: "It is me who, for penance, should expiate my sins. I am the cause of the whip and of all that you have suffered, o Lord! " This involvement of the churchgoer is expressed in so many beautiful arias and in many wonderful choral scenes throughout the work. Among the arias I remember the n. 18 ("I want to give you my heart"); the n. 29 ("With joy I will accept the cross and the cup, it is the cup where my Lord has drunk"); the n. 36 ("My Jesus, alas, is now lost"). Among the corals I recall the n. 21 ("Recognize, my guardian, take me with you, my pastor"); the n. 23 ("I want to stay here next to you"); the n. 31 ("Always happen what my Lord wants, his will is the best").

But let's come to the "heart" of the drama. Jesus, after the kiss of Judas (note the musically beautiful phrase of Jesus to Judah: "Friend, why did you come?"), is brought before the Sanhedrin and interrogated by Caiaphas. Meanwhile Peter entered the courtyard of the palace.

The evangelist tells (No. 45) that a servant approaches him. You hear the woman's voice: "You were also with Jesus of Galilee," and Peter's voice replies: "I don't know what you are talking about". Another servant approaches him and says: "This man also was with Jesus of Nazareth". Peter's voice responds indignantly: "I don't know that man" ("*Ich henne des Menschen nicht*"). Shortly afterwards others come to him and tell him (here the sentence is marked by the chorus): "You are certainly one of those; your way of talking betrays you". And Peter reacts again: "*Ich henne des Menschen nicht*". The Evangelist proceeds (n. 46): at that moment the rooster sang (*krähete der Hahn*); then Pietro thought about the words of Jesus (who had said to him, "Before the rooster sings you will deny me three times"), he went out and cried bitterly (*und ging heraus und weinete bitterlich*). Let's try to listen to this short passage several times to feel all its drama. Peter's voice, usually impetuous, is here secure in the three denials, but in his obstinacy he reveals holes of hesitation and uncertainty. At the rooster's song, tenderness towards the betrayed master has the upper hand: the words "*und ging heraus und weinete bitterlich*", with which the evangelist describes Peter's attitude, sends us a great emotion, because in them it is concentrated all the Peter's sorrow, his bitterness, his regret. That "*weinete*" (cried) is an intense vocalization in which weeping vibrates; and in that "*bitterlich*" (bitterly) it really encapsulates all the bitterness for the treachery just happened.

And at this point, the story is interrupted to give space to a meditative digression: it is an aria (n. 47) for an alto voice who, singing a melancholy melody, invokes: "Have mercy on me, Lord (*Erbarme Dich, mein Gott*), in the grace of my weeping; look at me: the heart and the eyes weep bitterly in front of you". He is the believer, who knows not to be different from Peter and asks for forgiveness of God of his own fragility and his daily betrayals. The melody of the violins is really the suggestion of a weeping, and it takes place on the pizzicato of the bass that evokes a choked sob. The choral n. 48 resumes the theme of sin and expresses the confidence that God's grace and mercy are far greater than sin.

Another point of great beauty is that of the judgment before Pilate. The dialogue between Pilate (who tries to save Jesus because he is convinced of his innocence) and the crowd (that insists to his crucifixion) is dramatic. Tremendous is the shout, you can say "wild", with which the crowd, interpreted by the choir, shouts: "Barabba", preferring the release of the assassin to the liberation of Christ (n. 54). Equally terrible is the shout of "Do crucify!" (*Lass ihn kreuzigen!*), with which the crowd ask Pilate for Jesus' death (still n. 54). "What bad action then did he?" Pilate asked (n. 56); the chorus promptly answers by speaking in the name of all the believers (n. 57): "He has done good to all of us. He gave sight to the blind, made the lame to walk, comforted the afflicted, raised sinners and charging on himself their faults. Nothing else did the Lord Jesus!". But the scream of the crowd prevails, and it is always that: "*Lass ihn kreuzigen!*" (n. 59). And it is an inhumane, barbarous, unmotivated scream that the music expresses with strong dissonance.

There is a theme that is the *leitmotif* of the *St. Matthew Passion*: it is a sweet theme, which appears in various chorals and that Bach has taken and reworked from an ancient Lutheran choral. The theme appears for the first time in choral n. 21; it reappears several times (for example, in n. 63: "O head covered with blood and wounds"); it acquires its most striking and evocative meaning immediately after the narration of Jesus' death (choral n. 72).

The moment of Jesus' death is another of the highest ones in the *St. Matthew Passion*. The evangelist tells us that by the ninth hour Jesus cried out loudly: *"Eli, Eli, lamma sabactani?"*. We hear the intense and majestic voice of Jesus (this time supported by the organ: it no longer has his aura played by strings), who cries his invocation to the Father. The evangelist translates the sentence into German. The crowd says: "He calls Elijah", and: "Let's see if he comes to set him free" (these two sentences, sung by the choir, are two short but extraordinary polyphonic constructions). Then the evangelist resumes: "But Jesus cried out loud again (*schriee abermal laut*) and expired (*und verschied*)". Let's note that *"verschied"*: the voice of the evangelist crushes and breaks. A moment of silence follows. Then the choir starts the choral n. 72: "When one day I'll go, don't leave me. When I'll have to face death, come and help me... Loosen me from my fears with the strength of what you have suffered". This sweet, whispered choral seems to gather and express the pain of the world; it is pervaded by that suspenseful and trembling sense that follows the end of every agony, when the body of the dead relaxes in serenity after the tension of suffering, and the bystanders are enfolded by the reflection on the mystery of death.

The death of Jesus is followed by the narration of the earthquake (n. 73). It is a very moving, figurative piece, in which music describes the phenomena told by the Gospel: the veil of the temple breaks, the earth trembles, the tombs open, the deads resurrect, the soldiers start to fear. In this moving passage, a contemplative pause suddenly opens; it is the centurion who shouts: "He truly was the son of God". That scream is expressed by the chorus, almost to symbolize that in the centurion all humanity is summed up: it is a slow, elaborated, polyphonic, almost ecstatic exclamation that relaxes and extends with distant echoes.

The *Passion* ends with the burial of Jesus, accompanied by a chorus that sings: "Good night, my Jesus" (*"Mein Jesu, gute Nacht!"*), alternating with soloists, ranging from the lowest voices to the highest voices in commenting the fulfillment of the salvation act. In that "Good night" there is a note of affectionate confidence, familiarity, intimacy, accompanied by the sweet awareness that a great deal of hard work has already been accomplished, that a tough task is now done. A monumental final choir concludes the opera singing "Rest in peace!" (*"Ruhe sanfte, sanfte ruh!"*): It is a chorus that acts as a symmetrical *pendant* with the initial chorus of the women of Jerusalem.

After Bach's death, the Bachian music was forgotten. Bach's discovery began right from the *St. Matthew Passion*. In the centenary of his first performance, that was in 1829, Felix Mendelssohn organized and directed a performance that took place in Berlin with a striking success. Since then, interest in Bach grew strongly; the researches of his compositions widened; the Bachian studies intensified; they discovered what immense genius was the modest Kantor of Leipzig.

Today, through the countless executions of the *Passion* that take place in the world, immense multitudes of listeners - believers and non-believers - are led by Bach's art to meditate on the passion and death of the one who is the nonviolent for excellence, the man who has lived his life as a being-for-others, without any limit or reserve.

The great Bach is even more contemporary than ever before: with the magisterium of his art, he offers to the today man a supreme message of nonviolence and love.

GETTING TO KNOW BACH

The numbering of Bach's works, commonly followed, is proposed by Wolfgang Schmieder for the general catalog of Bachian works. The abbreviation BWV is composed of the initials of the words *Bach Werke Verzeichnis*, meaning "Catalog of Bach works". Each Bachian composition is indicated by the BWV followed by a progressive number.

For a first approach to Bach, I used the book of Albert Schweitzer *Bach, il musicista poeta*, Suvini Zerboni, Milano 1952: it is a stimulating book in which the great doctor, an apostle of humanitarianism and enthusiastic organist, traced an effective profile of the musician, whom he was an admirer.

More recent and critically more modern biographies are those by Eduardo Rescigno, *Bach*, Fabbri, Milan 1980; by Loredana Lipperini, *Invito all'ascolto di Bach*, Mursia, Milan, 1984; by Helene Werthemann, *J. S. Bach. La vita, l'opera, la fede*, Queriniana, Brescia 1965; by Piero Buscaroli, *La nuova immagine di Bach*, Rusconi, Milan 1982, and - most recently - *Bach*, Mondadori, Milan 1988. In addition, the next, wider 1998 edition by Roland De Candé, *Johann Sebastian Bach*, Studio Tesi, Pordenone 1990; as well as: Christoph Wolff, *J. S. Bach, La scienza della musica*, Bompiani, Milan 2003; Ciro Raimo, *Le due anime di J. S. Bach*, in "Nuova Rivista Musicale Italiana", Rai Eri, April-June 2008, pages 177-204; Antonio Brena, *Le seduzioni di Bach*, Zecchini, Varese 2010.

The most extensive and complete Italian biography is by Alberto Basso, *Frau Musika: la vita e le opere di J.S. Bach*, EDT, Turin 1979-1983, a powerful two-volume study on the life and work of the great composer. By Basso is also useful to read *L'età di Bach e Händel*, EDT, Turin 1976.

Also interesting the essays: by Massimo Mila, *La vecchiaia di Bach*, Accademia delle scienze, Turin 1981; by Luigi Ronga, *Bach, Mozart, Beethoven. Tre problemi critici*, Venice 1956; and by Gianni Long, *J. S. Bach, il musicista teologo*, Claudiana, Turin, 1985. About the Bachs' "dynasty" can be seen the book by Karl Geiringer, *I Bach*, Rusconi, Milan 1984.

About specific works of Bach we can remember: Guglielmo Barblan, *Guida a Il Clavicembalo ben temperato di Bach*, Milan 1961; Luigi Ferdinando Tagliavini, *Studi sui testi delle cantate sacre di Bach*, CEDAM, Padua 1956; Luigi Perrachio, *Il Clavicembalo ben temperato di Bach*, Edizioni Palatine, Turin 1947; Jacques Chailley, *Les Passions de Bach*, PUF, Paris, 1963; Giorgio Pestelli, *La Passione secondo Giovanni di J. S. Bach. Problemi di analisi musicale. Con appendice di lettere*, Giappichelli, Turin 1973; Meredith Little and Natalie Jenne, *Dance and the Music of J. S. Bach*, Bloomington (USA) 1991; Meredith Little and Hermann Keller, *Il Clavicembalo ben temperato di Johannes Sebastian Bach. L'opera e la sua interpretazione*, Ricordi, Milano 1991; Pietro Ferrando, *Il «Preludio e fuga per organo» di Bach*, Trauben, Turin 2006; Alfred Dürr, *J. S. Bach's St. John's Passions Genesis*, Oxford University Press, 2000; Sergio Bianchi, Giuliano Bellorini and Paolo Beschi, *Le suites per violoncello solo di J. S. Bach. Analisi, storia, stile, prassi esecutiva*, LIM, Lucca 2008; Franco De Bernardi, *Bach. Le grandi opere corali*, Gribaudo, Milan, 1996; Heinrich Besseler, *Bach e il Medioevo*, in "Nuova rivista musicale italiana", 1985, from page 5; Roman Vlad, *Nei nomi di J. S. Bach e G. F. Händel*, same, from page 75; David Toro, *J. S. Bach, Dialoghi e divertimenti*, Zecchini, Varese

2005; Julius Osto, *Un pentagramma teologico. Musica e teologia nella cantata 140 di J. S. Bach*, Edizioni Messaggero, Padova 2010; Giulia Biagetti, *Johann Sebastian Bach 2000*, Associazione Musicale di Camaiore, Tipolito Editrice Modernografica, Lucca 2006, pages 11-32: on this volume there is also an interesting contribution by Alberto Basso, entitled *Frau Musika: vent'anni*.

A comparison between Bach and Händel can be seen in John Butt, *Bach e Händel: differenze entro una comune cultura dell'invenzione musicale*, in Enciclopedia della musica, edited by Jean-Jacques Nattiez, Einaudi, Turin 2004, vol. IV, pages 528-551.

Many valuable news on Bach's compositions can be found in *Storia della Musica* (The New Oxford History of Music), Feltrinelli / Garzanti, Milan 1991, vol. VI, from page 292 (*I concerti brandeburghesi*); 387 (*Bach e lo stile italiano*); 389 (*Bach e la forma del concerto*); 665 (*Le Variazioni di Bach*); 672 (*Le Partite di Bach*); 677 (*Il clavicembalo ben temperato*); 684 (*L'arte della fuga*); as well as an essay by Walter Kolneder on *Le Suites per orchestra di J. S. Bach* (from page 278). Finally, I recall two recent and very original biographies: Andrea Frova, *Bravo Sebastian. Dieci episodi nella vita di Bach*, Bompiani, Milano 2007 (publication that has the advantage of bringing the text of several letters written by Bach, but - in my humble opinion - the failure to contain several widely romanticized pages); Mario Ruffini, *Lo specchio di Dio e il segreto dell'immagine riflessa*, Edizioni Polistampa, Florence 2012 (very original and interesting book, since from the title and the foreword by Ramin Bahrami).

GEORG FRIEDRICH HÄNDEL
(1685-1759)

A firework of melodies and harmonies

Georg Friedrich Händel in a traditional portrait of an unknown author.

Händel was born in Halle on February 23rd 1685. Halle is in Saxony, East Germany; it is about 150 kilometers far from Eisenach, the birthplace of Bach. The two musicians were born in the same year, less than a month one from the other. It is then spontaneous to bring near their figures and examine them in parallel.

Contact points are many. Bach and Händel are the two "giants" of German music in the first half of the eighteenth century. Both were excellent performers of various instruments, formidable organists, open to all the trends of European music; both Lutherans; both - in old age - afflicted by blindness.

But their differences are very deep. Much different are the families in which they were born (Bach in a family of musicians, Händel in the family of a "cerusico", that is, a physician-surgeon of that time) and different are the studies that did (Bach only applied to musical studies and had rather obscure masters; Händel studied law at the University of Halle, where he had as a rector Christian Thomasius, a pioneer of Enlightenment, the first professor to teach in German rather than Latin, and in music he had a valiant master, Zachau. While Bach never went out from Germany, Händel traveled a lot in Europe and he met many musicians, especially Italians. While Bach never practiced the theater, Händel was an acclaimed composer of operas and also a manager of his own plays. Händel's fame had international echoes, while Bach's fame did not cross to the borders of Germany at that time.

These two great contemporaries never had the opportunity to meet. Twice Bach, having news of the passage in Halle by his famous colleague, tried to meet him, but came to the place when Händel had already left. The slowness of transport at that time and the absence of the phone frustrated twice Bach's good intentions, preventing a meeting that could have been of great importance in the history of music.

A RIGID FATHER AND A SYMPATHETIC DUKE

When Händel was born, his father - who had re-married after the death of his first wife - was sixty-four years old. He was a very rigid man and was very jealous of his prestige of "court-surgeon" at the duke of Saxony; he was opposed to the music, considering it to be of little dignity. He had the idea of making his son a law man; and when he noticed that he had musical inclinations, he forbade him to touch any instrument.

But little Georg had discovered an old harpsichord in the attic and he played it secretly. One day he run after his father's carriage bound to the duke's residence, he managed to reach it, and his father, touched by this act, get him to court, where a brother-in-law (born of his father's first marriage) was serving the duke. With the complicity of the brother-in-law, he managed to reach the organ of the court church, and taking advantage of the fact that the church was empty at the end of a religious function, he played the organ. But, for a singular and almost romantic combination, the duke was in the empty church at that time, and he was struck by the ability of the organ player and wanted to know the young organist. He then had an argument with his father and invited him to leave the boy free to follow his natural bias.

The father gave up the demands of the duke, and so Händel - as I said - came to the school of the organist Zachau: a rigorous but exciting school that provided the boy, then ten years old, a solid musical formation and steered him to the first compositions.

Later Händel, in respect of his father's will, who died in 1697, enrolled at the University of Halle; but shortly thereafter he was appointed organist of the Halle cathedral. He then decided to abandon his university studies and to fully devote himself to his artistic vocation, now clear and indisputable.

To instantly "tune us" on this great artist of the organ, we can listen to the first movement of the *Concert for organ and orchestra op. 4 n. 4*, composed some years later. We note that the organ is treated here as a solo instrument in dialogue with the orchestra; and that it is used not as a church instrument, but as a concert instrument. We then discover the brilliant resources of the organ, its gracefulness and its worldly joyfulness.

With Händel the stream of solo virtuosity begins; it will have with Johann Christian Bach (son of Johann Sebastian) and Wolfgang Amadeus Mozart its prodigious developments.

A TRAGICOMIC DUEL:
A SWORD BREAKS AGAINST A BUTTON

In 1703 Händel is in Hamburg. He is eighteen and is a violinist and harpsichord player in the orchestra of the city's theater. Hamburg is, at that time, the largest German music center. There Händel knows the musician Mattheson, with whom he develops a tempestuous friendship, made of sympathy and rivalry, which will also blow into a duel.

In fact, during the performance of the Mattheson's *Cleopatra* opera, Händel is playing the harpsichord; after the scene of Antonio's suicide, Mattheson (who has played the part of Antonio, who has definitely left the scene) goes to the harpsichord, to direct the rest of the work from there. But Händel opposes and does not allow it: he stays at the harpsichord. An brawl arises, which then degenerates into a duel.

A tragicomic duel because, despite the duelists are very ireful and determined to gut each other, Mattheson's sword breaks against a metallic button on the Händel jacket. The funny crash cools down the anger and everything ends up in a laugh and in a re-established friendship.

At that time, Händel and Mattheson went together in Lübeck to listen to the famous and old organist Buxtehude, an important experience that - as we have seen – also Bach had wanted to do. Both would like to compete for succession in the prestigious role of organist Marienkirche, but both of them (like Bach already) face the clause that forces the successor to marry the daughter of Buxtehude. And this is also a singular coincidence that unites the lives of Bach and Händel.

JOURNEY IN ITALY: «HAIL TO THE SAXON!»

In 1706 Händel left for Italy. In Hamburg he met the Florentine Gian Gastone de' Medici, who pushed him to go to Florence. In Florence, however, Händel finds a situation unfavorable to theater music, and therefore continues to Rome.

There he is welcomed with great sympathy and soon he becomes a guest of many Roman patrons. The Roman chronicles greet him with such phrases: "There has come to this city a Saxon, excellent cymbal player and composer". He holds concerts in the house of Cardinal Ottoboni; a poem by Cardinal Pamphili titles him as "a novel Orpheus". He knows Corelli, the two Scarlattis (Alessandro and Domenico), Pasquini.

About his relationship with Corelli there is an episode that is worth remembering, because it gives us an index of Händel's character. Corelli, a great violinist and composer, performs an ouverture of Händel, and the latter, not satisfied with the performance, grabs the violin out of his hands to show him how to perform the piece.

Händel's character is impetuous and angry; Corelli, however, responds with calm and courtesy: "But dear Saxon: this music is in the French style, which I do not understand". As you know, Corelli is a great master of the so-called "concerto grosso", that is a type of composition in which Händel will soon excel, treasuring Italian experiences.

To get closer to the Händel's "concerto grosso" we can listen to the second movement of his great op. 6 n. 2: the rigorous structural system, the melodic richness, and the variety of timbre colors give us the measure of Händel's concert art.

Rome is one of the capitals of the Italian opera. It is also the city where Giacomo Carissimi has worked intensively on the musical genre he is considered the founder of: the oratorio. Händel - who will widely practice the oratorio - draws from the Roman staying valuable experiences also in this field. But for Rome this period is not happy: in 1703 there was an earthquake in Lazio and people voted to give up to fun for five years. So the theatrical activity languishes and the opera, which is theater music, is severely affected. Moreover, they are times of war, and they fear a "plunder of Rome".

Händel goes back to Florence and performs the *Rodrigo* (his first opera in Italian language); then he returns to Rome and starts a service for the Marquis Francesco Ruspoli, for whom he composed the oratorio *La Resurrezione* (also in Italian). Then he travels to Venice in 1707; and as Venice is - at that time - much more musically alive than Rome, he goes back there in 1709, earning great success with the work *Agrippina,* whose performance is greeted with the ovation: "Hail to the Saxon!".

TWO CRUCIAL ENCOUNTERS

Several years pass and Händel increases sympathy for Italy. But in Venice he makes two encounters that will be decisive in his life. The first is with Ernesto of Hannover, brother of Duke of Hannover. The second encounter is with Duke of Manchester, Ambassador of England in Venice.

The first encounter makes Händel earn the role of Kapellmeister at the Duke Giorgio of Hannover. The second evolves in an invitation to London. And so in 1710 Händel settles in Hannover, with the intention of making a trip to England a few months later. Thus, with a solid job as Kapellmeister at the Hannover Court, Händel in 1711 leaves for England.

In London there is a very intense musical life. But after the death of Purcell (one of the greatest English composers, who died in 1695), there are no outstanding personalities in the music field. Therefore, Händel's personality is quickly raised. He writes *Rinaldo,* an Italian-style opera that, performed at the Haymarket theater, immediately reveals as a huge success.

Then Händel comes back, as promised, to Hannover. But the love for England remains very strong. The following year (1712) Händel comes back there with permission of Duke Giorgio to be there "for a reasonable time": that "reasonable time" will last forever, because Händel will settle in London and will no longer come back to Hannover.

We recalled two plays by Händel: *Agrippina* and *Rinaldo.* It is time, then, to "taste" a play by Händel. We could listen to one of these two. Or listen to *Alcina,* a work with chivalrous subject, inspired by the *Furious Orlando* story. The plot is - as is often the case in these works - very complicated, and is just a pretext for music. To get an idea of how the operas' melodies were, we could listen to the piece of Ruggiero *Verdi prati, selve amene,* a sweet theme of lyric-pastoral nature.

LONDON CITIZEN

Händel is perfectly acclimatized in London. He is first hosted by its patron Lord Burlington, in Piccadilly Street, one of London's most lively streets: still today that gorgeous street, which for some stretch runs along Green Park, is dominated by the imposing Burlington House, a sumptuous building that, even if later renovated, was already a noble and prestigious residence (later Händel will be living in Brook Street).

Through Lord Burlington, Händel makes countless friendships and fits into London's worldly life. One of the most curious and interesting friendships is that with a singular figure of musician: Thomas Britton, known as the "musical coal man" because he was a merchant of coal and, at the same time, a passionate viol player. With him Händel often and willingly played (Britton playing the viol, Händel playing the harpsichord), giving birth to very nice family evenings and rejoicing with good beer mugs.

Moreover, London was full of theaters: Haymarket, King's Theatre, Queen's Theatre, Covent Garden. And Händel, an experienced theater man, lived at his perfect ease. The fact that he had roots in London and had not came back to Hannover aroused the anger of Duke Giorgio, who became furious because the musician had break his word and had been unfair; he felt betrayed. Keep in mind that in those days the musician - as I have already told - was considered an employee, a member of the personnel. This made the rudeness Händel had directed to his employer even more serious and unforgivable.

Händel, however, does not worry too much about the wrath of his former master, and continues his ascent in the London life. He gets in good with Queen Anna and get a considerable salary. In 1713, at the conclusion of the Peace of Utrecht, he composes a monumental *Te Deum*, which is performed with great success in St. Paul's Cathedral and then repeated in the royal chapel of St. James; that *Te Deum* will become so appreciated and famous for replacing Purcell's *Te Deum* in the official English court ceremonies. How to say: Händel, a German musician, takes over Purcell, the greatest English musician of the time. This is indeed the sign that Händel has now become "English", for all intents. And British people begin to write his name with the spelling Handel, a word that in English pronunciation sounds like the German Händel.

We could, at this point, go back to the concerts for organ or to the "concerti grossi", and listen to some other gem of Händel's art. I would recommend the Concerto for organ op. 7 n. 1, whose last movement is a delightful *Allegro*.

AN INCREDIBLE TURN OF EVENTS...
BUT THEN WATER MELTS THE ICE

In the following year, however, in 1714, an incredible, paradoxical, really novelistic fact happened: that Duke Giorgio of Hannover, whom Händel had treated so incorrectly, unexpectedly becomes King of England with the name of George I. In fact, Queen Anne died without leaving direct heirs, and, according to the Act of Settlement, succession belongs to a distant relative of the deceased queen, relative who is just Giorgio of Hannover. It's an unpredictable turn of events, really worthy of a theater man who is Händel: reality overcomes fantasy.

It is easy to imagine the dismay of Händel, who suddenly finds as his king, and as his employer, just the one he severely offended, ungraciously turning his back.

And in fact for three years (or maybe a little less, according to some biographers), the relationship between the new king and the musician will be very cold, glacial. The king is deeply hostile: he does not even want to see him at court.

But then there will be a fact that will melt the ice of their relationships and restore friendliness. That fact is a party that takes place on the Thames on 17th July 1717 and for which Händel has written music and dances.

These are a series of pieces specifically composed to be performed outdoors, and indeed to be played on water (properly: on huge floating rafts on the Thames); this set of pieces is called, in fact, *Water Music*. This "music on water" is of a brilliant, overwhelming beauty; the king likes immensely; he asks to repeat it more and more, in the general blaze. *Water Music* conquers all of London; but above all it conquers the king. It can be said that water (the *Water Music* on the Thames) melted the ice that for years had characterized relations between Händel and King George I of England.

Let's listen to some of this *Water Music*: let's focus on the first movement (*Ouverture*), the fourth (*Minuetto*), on the sixth (an *Allegro* with evocative echoes of hunting horns), on the seventh (called *Hornpipe*, the name of a lively English dance). These are so famous pieces that we've probably already had the chance to hear them. Let us taste them all in their cool beauty, trying to put them in the historical frame that we have now remembered. Above all, we try to capture the "colors" of the timbral mixes. For example, in the first movement, there are noticeable bridges of timbres: the violins' voice (placed in the foreground, left-hand for those looking at the orchestra) binds with the trumpets' one (placed back and right-hand), while the dark voice of cellos and bass (located on the right) responds by combining with the tone of the horns (located on the left). A cross-game of contrasts, which gives particular liveliness and pleasure to the famous piece.

Since then Händel, consecrated court musician, will compose continuously, especially theater works (forty) in Italian language and Italian style: works of mythological subject (such as *Teseo*, or *Jupiter in Argo*), historical (such as *Silla, Muzio Scevola, Serse*) or chivalrous (like *Orlando, Ariodante* or the aforementioned *Alcina*). His production is a real firework. He will become a manager of his works and in that way he will travel a lot to organize the performances and to engage famous singers (especially Italians). The operas are written in Italian and the most sought after singers are Italian ones, because it is the era in which Italian opera is extremely successful all over Europe, and a theatrical performance in music can't be conceived if not written and sung in the Italian language.

To one of those works, the *Serse*, belongs the most famous and performed piece of Händel: the *Largo*. It is a melody that is often played in the church as a sacred melody for its sweet and solemn motif and for its intimacy gathering, but it was born as an theme for a theater work (the tune *Ombra mai fu*).
So let's listen to this well-known *Largo* di Händel.
Another beautiful *Largo* is *Ruhe und Friede* ("Rest and peace"), from the *Rinaldo* opera: it is based on a poetic text that expresses feelings of prayer; the slow and majestic pace of music widens and boosts those feelings.

A PORTRAIT WITH STRONG CONTRASTS

It may be interesting to sketch a Händel portrait.
A massive and corpulent figure; the paintings that give us his effigy reveal a wide face, solemnly framed by a long wig, typical of the era, and an imposing body. He was crude and imperative in the contours, impetuous and irrational, especially with capricious and overbearing people. It is reported that in the face of a singer,

Francesca Cuzzoni, who wanted to make him change the music to make her voice stand out, he resolutely refused, and - dazed by her insistence - took the woman out of the window, dangling, holding her by the neck with his strong arms and shouting that he would have let her fall down if she had continued in her whims. Not all versions of the episode coincide, but it is certain that Händel threatened the singer to throw her down the window and gestured to throw her away.

That impetuous temper, however, was devoid of badness or malice. His friends talked of his wide, bright smile as a ray of sunshine emerging from a black cloud: it was not, therefore, capable of holding the brunt. He was ready for wit and inclined to humor. He was a talented and loving narrator. His biographers tell that he knew how to make people laugh, without laughing, that is a perfect humorist talent. In his activity he was tireless, and they remembers that he once played uninterruptedly from 7 to 11, without showing signs of fatigue. He was a painting connoisseur and loved Rembrandt, the great Dutch painter of the seventeenth century.

He did not get married, and nothing is known about his sentimental life; it was locked in absolute privacy, which no biographer could scrap. It is only known about his sympathy, arisen in 1706 in Pratolino (Florence) for Vittoria Tarquini, a court lady of the Grand Duke of Tuscany.

Lutheran Christian, he had deep religious convictions: in fact he could write sacred music, characterized by an authentic and vibrant religious spirit (of which we will see a few examples). When he was proposed to abjure, for convenience, his Lutheran faith, he rejected with disdain. He did not become Catholic in Rome, as he did not become Anglican in England.

Concerning the spirit with which he composed his sacred music, it is enough to recall a sentence he said about the Messiah: "I would be sorry if I had just entertained the audience. I would have made it better". But some (such as Swanston) doubt that the musician has really pronounced that sentence: indeed, according to the commentator, the Lutheran conception of man's improvement and salvation is the work of God, not of men. But, in my humble opinion, such a conception does not exclude at all that man can and must cooperate with God's action.

I would say that just that religious spirit is, beside other factors, the key point of an extraordinary breakthrough in Händel's art. Towards 1730 in England there is a sense of saturation about Italian opera, or anyway of Italian-style opera. And indeed, Italian opera is a type of composition that has made its time: it is now a tired and empty repetition of conventional schemes. Its characters are historical or mythological figures far away from reality, with no human thickness. The structure of the opera has fossilized in a sequel of arias and recitations built above all to allow singers to do singing stunts and to exalt the public with the so-called 'beautiful song', reduced to a sort of competition: there are fans of singer X and fans of singer Y... It is, in short, a degeneration of the opera.

Even in Italy, a homeland of this kind of music, a new type of opera is emerging, drawn from everyday life and fueled by popular moods: Pergolesi is creating a musical "comedy of art"; comic opera is supplanting the serious opera; in 1733 appears *La serva padrona*, the very first Italian comic opera. In England the declinating Italian opera, sung in Italian, is surrendering to a folk music opera, sung in English: the Beggar's Opera by John Gay and Peputsch. The decline of the Italian opera also has an impact on Händel, who experiences failure and economic disaster. With great insight he understands that it is time to beat other streets and he moves towards the oratorio (that is, the religious composition) sung in English. The English people know the Bible very well; and biblical subjects will now become the favorite for Händel. He is not Anglican, as the English are: he is a German Lutheran; but his religious faith draws on the same biblical sources as the Anglican faith. The common biblical-Christian root allows the encounter of the new course of Händel's music with the palate of English people.

Though the oratorio is a composition that is performed without stage action and without theatrical effects, Händel does not stop to be a theater man, and brings into the biblical oratorio an intense theatrical dramatization, in which he gives the choir an essential and leading role.

The first oratorio is *Esther*, which is performed in Oxford in 1733, as part of a Händel's music festival in which the *Te Deum* of

Utrecht is also included. A big success. They will follow *Deborah*, *Saul*, *Israel in Egypt*, *Samson* and many more.

But in 1737 Händel's fervent activity undergoes a halt: a paralysis immobilizes his right arm. His strong fiber overcomes his illness; he can recover and start composing again. And in 1741 he created a great masterpiece, the *Messiah*, which is one of the great peaks of his art. It is a musical fresco that illustrates, in terms of religious meditation, the story of Jesus, which embodies the Messiah prophesied by the Old Testament, the expected Savior of all peoples.

The *Messiah* is performed for the first time in Dublin in 1742 and provokes genuine enthusiasm: the room in which it is performed is expected to be so full that the organizers recommend ladies to go without hoops at skirts (they used very large skirts, supported by large hoops) and men to go without a sword in order to leave more space available. This gives the measure of the great expectation surrounding this musical event and the great success that the *Messiah* met.

The performance was repeated at Covent Garden in London: the *Alleluja* is so majestic and thrilling that the king, impulsively, stood up at the first bars, and all the audience stood up with him. Since then, the habit has been used - very rooted in England, but spread all over the world and today in decline - to listen to the *Alleluja* standing, in reverence and admiration toward this great musical page and to the very high sentiments that it expresses.

Let us listen to this imposing *Alleluja*. On this word, which is the typical Easter acclamation (*Hallelu* means "Praise", *Ja* is the abbreviation of Jahwè, which is the Jewish name of God, so "Praise God"), Händel constructs a great polyphonic masterpiece. It expresses with explosive force the unbreakable joy of the extraordinary news: Christ is risen. I will make an analysis of it at the end of this chapter.

SUMMIT AND DECLINE. TOWARDS THE «POETS' CORNER»

Another significant moment in the life of Händel is 1749. The Aachen Peace was the year before, and London celebrates the event with a great festival of fireworks at Green Park.

For the occasion Händel is invited to write a composition, and composes a number of pieces called *Fireworks*. Crowding and success are such that carriages create a queue that extends from

Green Park to the London Bridge, also filling it for its entire length. A memorable event at that time.

Let's listen to at least one of the pieces that make up *Fireworks*. I would recommend listening to the first one: the *Overture*.

The activity of the musician continues in the following years. But in 1751 (the year after Bach's death), Händel is affected by eye disease during the composition of the oratorio *Jefte*. He is taken care of by the most illustrious ophthalmologists of the time (Sharp and Taylor: the latter is the surgeon who operated Bach) but his vision continues to deteriorate and in 1753 he becomes totally blind. However, he still plays organ and still manages to compose with the help of friends.

He died on April 14th 1759, on Holy Saturday while bells of *Gloria* are playing. He had always said that he wanted to die on Easter day, the day of Jesus' resurrection.

It is Easter Eve: in the liturgy of that time the Mass of the Holy Saturday anticipates that of Easter and the moment of *Glory* is exactly when the community of believers celebrates and revives the resurrection of his Lord.

In his will, Händel asked to be buried in Westminster abbey in private form. His tomb lies in Westminster, in the so-called Poets' Corner, located in the right transept of the church. It is next to the tombs of Shakespeare, Milton, Chaucer, Walter Scott and other greats of English art and literature: almost to point out once again that England has become its second homeland.

On his funeral monument are carved the words of a passage from the *Messiah*: "I know that my Redeemer lives ..."

It is a tribute to his music and also to his Christian faith, matured in the womb of the ancient Lutheran church of Saxony.

LISTENING GUIDE TO A MASTERPIECE: THE MESSIAH

The *Messiah* is a great musical fresco in the form of an oratorio, which presents some pictures relating to the life of the Lord Jesus (the Messiah, in fact).

Unlike the Passions, which have the gospel background as the backbone, the *Messiah* is not set to a story. It consists of a series of detached musical paintings, designed to offer a trace of meditation on the fundamental stages of Christ's life and mission. For this reason Alberto Basso prefers to speak of "polyptych" rather than "fresco".

There is, therefore, no "narrator" who drains the thread of his tale by providing the connective tissue of the work. No. Here the connective tissue is only provided by various pieces of the Old and New Testament, cleverly brought near.

For example, the birth of Jesus is seen through the prophecies of Isaiah; the passion and death of Jesus are seen through a "collage" of prophetic pieces from Jeremiah, Isaiah and from psalms; the famous *Alleluja* is built on some verses of the Apocalypse (the last book of the Bible, also called Revelation); the triumph of Christ is described through verses drawn from the various letters of St. Paul.

This oratorio became vary famous and was considered a symbol and a monument to the Western culture. There was, indeed, a tendency to emphasize it beyond all limits, to make it a giant: its execution widened to ever-expanding complexes, up to involve several thousand performers. It was an expression of the triumph of choral music, at a time when such a type of music passed from the closed-mindedness of court and church elites to the spread of popular classes. Today, they tend to go back to performances proportionate to Händel's times, to rediscover the size of its style, to work with greater fidelity to its conception.

The oratorio is divided into three parts. Händel composed it with impetus in only twenty-four days. The text, by Charles Jennens, is in English.

The first part is devoted to the birth of Jesus and the prophecies that announced it. It opens with an introductory symphony; then the tenor invites, in Isaiah's words, to prepare the way for the Lord to come. Other Isaiah's prophecies follow, now sung by the tenor, now by the soprano, now by the choir. Then the chorus explodes in the festive song: "Behold, a child was born, a son was given to us; on his shoulders he has the primacy and she will be called Admirable Counselor, Powerful God, Eternal Father, Prince of Peace" (*For unto us a Child is born, unto us a Son is given*). It is the prophecy of Isaiah (9,6). The chorus begins with a mild, frisky voice of joy talking about the child; then gradually enlarges and grows, becomes majestic and solemn with the words: Wonderful, Counselor, The Mighty God, The Everlasting Father, The Prince of Peace!

Following this chorus is a pastoral orchestral passage: it is referred to as the *Pastoral Symphony*, and Händel called it *Pifa* (probably from the Italian "piva", that is bagpipe, pronounced to German: "pifa"). This orchestral piece is dedicated to the musical meditation on the mystery of Christmas. Then the soprano, singing some verses of Luke's Gospel, briefly tells the announcement of the angels to the shepherds, followed by the beautiful and choral " Glory to God in the highest, and peace on earth, good will towards men!" (with the meaning of "Peace to men whom God loves").

The second part is devoted to the passion, death and resurrection of Jesus. As I have said, passion is recalled through prophetic and psalmist passages. It is well known that Isaiah, seven hundred years before Jesus, spoke of the passion of the "servant of Jahwé", describing it with details that impressively coincide with the passion of Jesus. It is also known that certain psalms fit perfectly with the story of Christ.

Passion goes to the resurrection through the song of the soprano, which says: "But you will not abandon his soul in the sepulcher, you will not allow the Saint to experience corruption" (Psalm 16), and through the choir song, which says: "Get up, doors, the king will come in" (Psalm 24); the resurrection is celebrated with the famous choir of the *Alleluia*, I have already mentioned. The text is a series of verses of the Revelation and points out the phrase: "King of Kings, and Lord of Lords, and He will reign for ever and ever."

The third part is devoted to the second coming of Jesus in the glory and to the resurrection of the dead. In this part it should be noted the soprano air *I know that my Redeemer liveth*, words taken from the book of Job (19,25), one of the books of wisdom in the Bible. The text of the oratorio adheres admirably to the words of Saint Paul in the first letter to the Corinthians: "But behold, Christ is risen from the dead, the firstborn of those who sleep in the grave" (1 Corinthians 15,20). The melody, very sweetly, expresses faith in Christ, who is a living being because, first of all men, has risen from death.

Following this melody there is a choir whose text is also drawn from the first letter of Paul to the Corinthians (15,21-22): "As for a man (Adam) death came, so for a man (Christ) the resurrection came". These are four verses: the first is sung in whispers, the second loudly, the third again quietly and the fourth very aloud. It is a chiaroscuro of extraordinary effectiveness. Those three moments (*Alleluja*, *I know that my Redeemer liveth* and *As for a man*) are so closely related and so express the joy of the Christian message that I call them the "triptych of joy".

It follows a "collage" of Pauline pieces, drawn from both the first letter to the Corinthians and the letter to the Romans, and sung now by the soloists, now by the choir. Then the oratorio ends with a piece of great polyphony, sung on the words of the Revelation: "The Lamb that has been killed is worthy of receiving power, wealth, wisdom, strength, honor, glory, praise. To God who is seated on the throne and on the Lamb is praise, honor, glory and power in the centuries of the centuries" (Revelation 5,12-13). This choral piece closes with a monumental fugue on the Hebrew word *Amen* (which means: "Yes, so it is!").

GETTING TO KNOW HÄNDEL

The commonly used numbering of Händel's works is very weak. It only concerns some groups of instrumental compositions: for example, two sets of "concerti grossi" are referred to as op. 3 and op. 6, two collections of concerts for organ and orchestra as op. 4 and op. 7, a collection of sonatas for solo instrument as op. 1, etc.

An organic collection of Händel's *opera omnia* was initiated and conducted by Friedrich Chrysander (died in 1904): it is not a real catalog, but its ninety-nine volumes constitute an important reference point, which is indicated by the initials HW (Händel Werke = Händel works).

A real catalog was edited by Bernd Baselt and it is quoted with the HWH acronym (Händel Werke Verzeichnis = catalog of Händel's works): but the use of its numbering is still not very common.

Few are Händel's biographies written in Italian or translated into Italian. Two Italian biographies were published in 1985: Guido Barbieri and Andreina Bonanni, *Händel, la vita e l'opera*, Newton Compton, Rome 1985; Gabriella Mazzola Nangeroni, *Invito all'ascolto di Händel*, Mursia, Milan 1985.

In 1985 (the 300th anniversary of Händel's birth), two important Italian translations were published: one of Händel's first biographies, released in English in London in 1760: John Mainwaring, *Memorie e vita del fu G. F. Händel*, EDT, Turin 1985 (republished by EDT in 2009, on the 250th anniversary of Händel's death); and that of a massive biography released in English in New York in 1966: Paul Henry Lang, *George Friedrich Händel*, Rusconi, Milan 1985. Lastly, Hamish Swanston, *L'ispirazione evangelica di Händel*, Claudiana, Torino 1992, with an essay by Long on the *Messiah*; Winton Dean, *Händel*, Ricordi / Giunti, Florence 1987; Christopher Hogwood, *G.F. Händel*, Studio Tesi, Pordenone 1991; John Butt, *Bach e Händel: differenze entro una comune cultura dell'invenzione musicale*, in Encyclopedia of Music, edited by Jean-Jacques Nattiez, Einaudi, Torino 2004, vol. IV, from page 528.

Numerous news about Händel's life and work can be found in the fundamental work of Alberto Basso, *L'età di Bach e di Händel*, EDT, Turin 1976.

Various Händel compositions (with particular regard to oratories, harpsichord music, and solo sonata) are described in the sixth volume of The New Oxford History of Music, Feltrinelli/Garzanti, Milan 1991, *passim*.

A short paragraph devoted to Händel's joyous Christianity is available in my book *Ascoltare l'Assoluto. Musica classica e annuncio cristiano*, third edition, Effatà, Cantalupa 2010, from page 49.

FRANZ JOSEPH HAYDN
(1732 - 1809)

A cheerful and humorous architect of sound shapes

Franz Joseph Haydn in a portrait by Ludwig Guttenbrunn, about 1770.

Franz Joseph Haydn was born in 1732 in Rohrau, a small town in Burgerland, an eastern region of Austria which borders on Hungary and which already has certain characteristics of the Hungarian puszta. Second son of twelve children, he lived a serene childhood in a country house with a thatched roof, in which the modesty of the environment was accompanied by a very lively sense of cleanliness, order and diligence while working.

His father was a carter, his mother was a cook. His father, like his grandfather, was delighted to play the harp, without knowing the musical notes. The serene atmosphere and the pleasure of "family music" were the base of a sense of optimism in Franz Joseph's personality and the occasion of a first contact with the musical feel.

At five, Franz Joseph goes to Hainburg and visits a cousin who is a school and singing teacher in the parish; the cousin, becoming aware of the qualities of the child, persuades his parents to leave him there for some time, in order to introduce him to music. The invitation is accepted and Franz Joseph stays there: he studies with strict methods and returns hospitality with small services such as, for example, ringing the bells.

During the preparation of a village festival, enlivened by music performed by students of the school, the timpanist (i.e. the timpani player) falls ill. Little Joseph (in German: Sepperl), who has a sense of rhythm and has a good possession of the rudiments of music, is in charge of replacing the sick player. Sepperl practices for many days, building a rudimentary drum with a sieve and a duster. The long and diligent exercises are successful: the concert is successful and the little timpanist is very much celebrated. Sepperl is six years old.

Let's immediately "taste" the music of the future composer. We can listen to some of his symphonies in which the timpani plays an important role: for example, the Symphony n. 100, called *The military*, in which the timpani is mush present in the second movement; or the Symphony n. 103, called *Drumroll*, whose beginning is characterized by a kettledrum played in «pianissimo». These performances of the kettledrum recall, with tenderness, the "debut" of Sepperl, as a six-year-old timpani player.

At that time Georg Reutter, Kapellmeister at the Cathedral of Vienna, is in Hainburg: he is visiting towns and countryside in search of new white voices to expand the choir of St. Stephen's Cathedral in Vienna. He hears Sepperl singing and chooses him to be part of the choir.

It is 1740. For Franz Joseph the opportunity opens to follow, in Vienna, music courses, to participate in choral performances, to know and practice directly the best music of the time.

The discipline of little singers, often exploited to the limit of their possibilities, is very hard. But Franz Joseph resists, animated by his passion for music and supported by a strong sense of humor and joke. One of the Haydn's feature is already looming: the taste of the joke. A very well known prank he did was to a chorus singer singing in the row in front of him, to which he cut the tail of the wig with scissors.

When his voice changed its tune and began to "croak" assuming a virile tone, Franz Joseph was asked to be castrated. At that time castration was, unfortunately, very practiced in order to maintain the sharp register of the male voice and to ensure the presence of male singers with soprano voices on the theater scenes. It was an inhumane practice that exploited and sacrificed the person's sexual dimension for utilitarian purposes of theatrical and musical career.

Haydn refused the ignoble proposal, with great dignity. No longer able to be part of a chorus of white voices, he was fired and had to face the problems of life in the great unknown Vienna.

GAG COMICS AND MUSICAL DIVE

It was not easy to find a job. Haydn began to fend for himself, agreeing to play the violin in public places, in church or even on the street. He not only played but also sang, an activity in which he was helped by the choir experience done in the choir of the Cathedral. He even sang at the Mariazell sanctuary, one of the most famous and frequented Marian shrines in Austria.

At that time, then, they used to organize small musical entertainments on the streets, sometimes originating from some particular occasion, such as, for example, celebrating a certain person in front of his home. Those entertainments were called "serenades" or "entertainments" or "cassations" (the word "cassation" derives from the German word *gasse*, which means "street", and indicates street entertainment).

Haydn participated in those entertainments not only as a performer, playing the violin, but also as a composer, because he often composed himself the music for the event.

And during one of those "serenade", taking place in front of the house of the comic actor Kurtz, known as Bernardon, beloved by the Viennese, Haydn was noticed: his music pleased the actor, who proposed him to compose accompanying music for some comic gags that he played in the theater. Thus, for example, the actor mimed a fall into the water and Haydn invented a music that effectively accompanied the skit with the sounds.

The experiment succeeded. Haydn was hired by Kurtz and composed the music for a comedy show that was called *Il diavolo zoppo* and which constituted a satire of serious Italian opera. The combination Kurtz-Haydn worked and Haydn began to make himself known. Unfortunately, however, the show was then banned by the imperial police because the Empress Maria Theresa did not allow the Italian opera, a favorite at court, to be ridiculed, becasue consequently it could be ironic about the director of the imperial theaters.

Kurtz had to leave Vienna, and Haydn found himself jobless again.

We discovered Haydn's comical vein: his music is often full of jokes, surprises, onomatopoeic sounds (that is imitative of noises and voices of nature). So we anticipate the knowledge of the symphony n. 82, which is commonly known under the designation of *The Bear*. In fact it seems to us that the music evokes, especially in the last movement (Finale vivace) the clumsy and cute animal. This movement is based on a characteristic popular theme, whose accompaniment, performed with the bass, has a trend full of "acciaccature" that recalls the heavy and awkward gait of the bear.

LUCKYNESS IS NAMED «PORPORA»

Evicted from the flat that he occupied, Haydn managed to settle in an attic of a building not far from the church of San Michele: it was a small and cold attic, where he spent hours studying at the harpsichord, working until late at night.

For a very lucky combination, the famous Metastasio, an Italian poet who had settled in Vienna and had become a court poet with the Habsburgs, lived in that same building. The poet began to feel curiosity and interest in the skinny young man he sometimes met on the stairs and who played the harpsichord till the early hours; and when he hosted at his home during his stay in Vienna Nicolò Porpora, an Italian friend, one of the most famous composers of the time, told him about this strange boy.

Porpora wanted to know the young man, and found in him some musical genius. He gave him advice and ended up proposing to become his student and assistant. Haydn accepted. That role turned out to be very heavy indeed, because Porpora had a rather authoritative and irascible temper; but he offered Haydn the opportunity to meet musicians and poets, nobles and courtiers both in Vienna and in the spa town of Mannersdorf: among the most famous acquaintances, the famous composer Gluck.

It was, for him, a melting pot of musical experiences, coming both from the German area and from the Italian area. Thus the first quartets were born, among with the first concerts and the first symphonies. And a network of important relationships was born, which introduced Haydn into the world of Viennese nobility and high society.

I propose to listen to a beautiful *Concerto for trumpet and orchestra in E-flat major*. Haydn wrote it in later times, but it is worthwhile to hear it at this point because it immediately gives us the measure of the setting of a Haydnian concert and its clear melodic vein. I recommend to hear the first and third movement. The latter is very lively, and there are those who see a comic mood, as if Haydn wanted to mimic the Italian opera buffa, which had been born a few years before with *La serva padrona* by Giovanni Battista Pergolesi.

Un musicista in livrea

In 1761 Haydn finally found a stable professional and economic arrangement: he was hired as deputy Kapellmeister by Prince Paolo Antonio Esterházy, the most powerful Hungarian gentleman. Hungary was then part of the Habsburg Empire, and the prince lived in a beautiful castle in Eisenstadt (Austria) and in summer moved to the summer residence of Esterházy (Hungary). The court musicians received, according to the habits of the time, the same treatment received by the various members of the servants. They had to wear a special service uniform (the "livery"); they ate meals with the servants; they had to compose music according to the orders and tastes of the prince; they could not give their compositions to anyone (they did not have any copyright and their works were of the master's exclusive property).

It is interesting to read some clauses of the contract, since they give us the measure of what the social status of the musician was:

"When the orchestra is called to perform in society, the vice-Kapellmeister and all the musicians will appear in livery and the said Joseph Haydn will have to watch over so that he and all the members of the orchestra follow the prescribed rule and appear in white stockings, white knitwear, powdered, both with pigtail hair and knotted wig... The vice-Kapellmeister will have the obligation to compose all kinds of music commanded by His Serene Highness, and not to give such compositions to anyone else».

So the musician is at the same level as the gardener, the cook or the groom: he has the task of providing a certain performance, with certain modalities, on occasions and times that depend exclusively on the will of the master. It does not matter that the musician has or has no inspiration: if there is a party or a show or a concert, he must provide the music necessary for the occasion. Music composed on command; music to be functional at a certain event; music as consumer goods, which becomes the exclusive property of the master.

But even in this condition of absolute dependence, Haydn finds himself in a privileged situation for a composer: that of having an orchestra available every day, and therefore to have an ideal environment for musical experimentation. Something similar to what had happened, a few decades before, to Vivaldi, even if he had enjoyed greater artistic freedom.

After about a year Prince Paolo Antonio dies, and his brother Nicola succeeds to him. This is a refined man, music lover, inclined to grandeur. They call him «Il Magnifico». In Esterházy, he builds a magnificent palace, with a theater with five hundred seats, located on the southern shore of Lake Neusiedl. He raises up the number of the orchestra players and Haydn is promoted to Kapellmeister.

The residence in Esterházy will be favored by Prince Nicola, who will tend to dwell there, every year, for as long as possible, causing discontent in servants and orchestra players, forced to stay away from families for a long time.

And so, one day, Haydn gives voice to that protest, writing a symphony with which he intends to make the prince understand that it is time to leave Esterházy. The symphony begins with the whole orchestra; then, as the symphony proceeds, various groups of musicians turn off the candle of their music stand and move away, ceasing to play. In this way the voice of the orchestra is thinning and becoming more and more thin, until at last only two violins remain, with which the symphony ends.

The prince understands the witty musical symbology and welcomes the requests of his musicians. The symphony is the n. 45; it was composed in 1772 and bears the significant title *Abschiedsymphonie* (Symphony of farewell).

Let's listen to it. The first movement is a very, impetuous, stormy *Allegretto*, in the style of *Sturm und Drang*; the second movement is a very plaintive *Adagio*. The third movement is a *Minuetto*; the fourth movement has a fast start, which is replaced by an *Adagio* (unusual for a last movement). And it is here that the joke played by Haydn to the prince takes place. First of all, this *Adagio* repeats to infinity a slow and plaintive theme: it gives a sense of monotony, of boredom, almost expressing the monotony of repetitiveness and the surfeit of routine. Then, after thirty-one bars played together by all the instruments, the first oboe and the second horns leave. Shortly after, the bassoon leaves, then the second oboe, after which the first horns, the double-basses and the cellos are gone; then the two groups of violins; then the violas. At the end there are only two first violins, that play with the mute, more and more weakly. With these two violins only the singular symphony ends. It ends, I would say, fading out.

This is a very fruitful time for Haydn. His compositions are multiplied: symphonies, concerts, dances, quartets, masses, theater works. In essence, that intense productivity is expressed above all in three main streams: theatrical productions, sacred music, instrumental music. About this last stream (which was the most practiced by Haydn) I would suggest listening to the last time of *Concerto for horn n. 4* (Hob. VII d / 4), which seems to me full of original passages;

among other things, the horn was the favorite instrument of Prince Nicola.

I would suggest that you also listen to the last part of the *Concerto for horn n. 3*. It seems less original than the previous one, but has the characteristic of being rich in virtuosic passages. Not for nothing, it seems that Haydn wrote it for the skilled hornist Steinmüller. Among other things, we can remember that the original score of this concert is full of corrections and that in the last two pages Haydn has even exchanged the two upper lines, probably for the hurry. He then wrote in the margin: "Composed while I was sleeping". Another nice example of his humor, which here is expressed in self-irony. This concert is listed as Hob. VII d / 3.

AN EVENTFUL SENTIMENTAL LIFE

Meanwhile, in 1760, Haydn had married. He had initially fallen in love with Teresa Keller, the daughter of a wig maker, in whose family he went to give music lessons. He had asked her parents to marry the girl, but Teresa had previously decided to become a nun, and the young man had not been able to carry out his marriage project.

The biographies say that at this point the Keller parents had maneuvered to make him marry Teresa's older sister Maria Anna, and that Haydn had ended up accepting. According to the biographers, an unhappy marriage was born: Maria Anna turned out to be a capricious, shrewish, spendthrift wife, denied for music (she even used her husband's musical manuscripts to become "curlers"); an infernal conjugal life derived from it, which had led to a separation.

It is not unlikely that Haydn had his blames in the bad relationship with his wife. Moreover, the fact that she could not have children probably constituted a crisis factor. And, on the other hand, in the strongly masculine age, in which the current mentality admitted and justified for man wide and unilateral freedoms in terms of conjugal fidelity, it is not unlikely that Haydn himself gave rise to conjugal contrasts.

It is also known that the musician had more than a fleeting passion and that, after the separation, he established a relationship, which lasted a long time, with the singer Luigia Polzelli. With another woman, Maria Anna Sabina von Genzinger, Haydn had instead a very different kind of relationship: a very correct and devoted friendship, which inspired him more than one composition. The woman was the wife of the court physician, she had a strong musical sensibility, and with her husband she worked very hard to make the compositions of the master known and appreciated in Vienna.

For the monastic dressing of Teresa, Haydn wrote a concert for organ and orchestra (Hob. XVIII n. 1). We would expect a concert of a religious type, given the circumstance and the nature of the solo instrument (organ). Instead, Haydn treats the organ in a "profane" way, in the style of Händel, and presents us with a brilliant composition, where there is no trace of sadness or even religious meditation. It seems that even in the suffering of detachment from the beloved, Haydn senses that even the choice of monasticism, perfectly free and not imposed, as sometimes happened at that time, can be a choice of joy and life when it is the result of deep conviction and full adherence to the Gospel values: one should think of St. Francis of Assisi or, here being a woman, St. Clare and the joy of the religious choices of one and the other.

FROM THE «CONCERTO GROSSO» TO THE « SONATA FORM». AN EXTRAORDINARY «CHESS PLAYER»

As I have already said, for Haydn the service at Esterházy opens a long and very productive period. In the immense production of this period we find a central vein that concerns a decisive turning point in the history of music: the birth of the sonata form, that is a formal scheme that will constitute the essential structure of the symphony, the quartet, the concert for solo instrument and orchestra, of the piano sonata, of the sonata for piano and violin, for piano and cello, and so on.

To explain the value of this formal scheme, Massimo Mila compares it to what in the literature is the octave (think of the harmonious octaves by Ariosto or Tasso) or the sonnet (think of the sonnets by Foscolo).

Basically, we pass from the "concerto grosso", built on the contraposition of instrumental blocks (the so called "concertino" and the "tutti" or "filled"), to a more subtly articulated type of composition, based on the dynamics of two themes (in different tones) that are both exposed and that become the protagonists of the composition; these themes are developed through various modulations and finally restated in the main key, with which the piece ends.

In this way the sonata form is movement, is history, is a dramatic action carried out by exquisitely musical characters (the themes) that do not remain the same but continually change, develop, walk, compare, dialogue, in a continuously changing reality. This reality becomes richer and more dazzling as it enhances the variety of orchestral tones in a more organic and penetrating way. The dynamics of the composition is no longer based on a mere contraposition between "concertino" and "tutti", but is based on a thematic juxtaposition, greatly enriched by the timbre peculiarities of the various instrument families and therefore by a kind of instrumental polyphony.

Here then the symphony, the sonata, the concert, all structured according to an architecture of which Haydn is considered the "father". The symphony (composition for orchestra) is definitely settling in four movements: usually an *Allegro*, an *Adagio* or *Andante*, a *Minuetto*, a final *Presto*. The sonata (composition for harpsichord, organ or piano alone, or composition for a single instrument accompanied by harpsichord, organ or piano) and the concert (composition for solo instrument and orchestra) are settling in three movements: a joyful movement, a second slow movement, a quick third movement (*Allegro* or *Presto*).

It should be noted, however, that this "point of arrival" is not the exclusive fruit of Haydn's genius, but is also the result of a long maturation, which lasted centuries and required the travails of many musicians of different ages and nationalities.

Nor can it be said that Haydn is the rigid codifier of the sonata form. In fact, even if he arrives at that kind of musical architecture, he does not remain a prisoner of absolute and imperative rules: he maintains full creative freedom, sometimes derogating himself from the rules he has drawn. As stated by Giovanni Carli Ballola, his game is similar to that of the great chess player: free, creative, unpredictable and yet rigorously organized.

If we listen to any instrumental composition of Haydn's maturity, we find clear the schema of the sonata form, albeit used with the freedom mentioned above. If we want a particular example, we can take the first movement of the *Symphony n. 83*, called *La Gallina* for the rhythm that, in the first movement, characterizes the second theme, evoking realistically the voice of the hen.

The innate sense of humor of Haydn and his tendency to joking appear in his music and especially in his symphonies. Not surprisingly, the latter sometimes have curious and strange titles, some of which are given by Haydn himself, others given by publishers.

András Schiff, pianist and orchestra conductor, highlights in one of his writings that the hallmark of Haydn's humor is the juxtaposition of expectations and surprises, of conventional and unconventional, of symmetry and asymmetry, as well as the use of unusual sound effects, the game with silence and rythm, the drastic dynamic contrasts.

We have already seen how Haydn played a tasty musical joke to Prince Esterházy with the *Farewell Symphony*.

We can now remember the Symphony n. 94, called *The Surprise* or *The Kettledrum Stroke*, in whose second movement, after a slow and pianissimo beginning by the strings, suddenly a strong tympanic blow is an unexpected surprise: Haydn himself said he had wanted, with that blow, to catch listeners to surprise and make them jump on chairs, as to prevent them from drowsing and drawing their attention.

Or the *Symphony n. 60*, called *The Distracted*, in whose last movement the orchestra seems, at a certain point, to lose itself and not to know how to continue: it started resolutely, and now suddenly whispers in an embarrassing silence; it seems disoriented, and emits some tearing dissonances, similar to those of an orchestra tuning the instruments; then, suddenly, that mess ceases and the orchestra resumes playing in perfect accord, as if nothing had happened, intoning a beautiful folkloric melody and bringing the symphony to conclusion.

A similar joke is found in the quartet op. 74 n. 3 (called *The Rider* because in the last movement it evokes horse trot with a strict musical texture in which respect for rules and creative imagination are wonderfully combined): a delightful construction for the thematic richness and the liveliness of rhythm; a very pleasant and exciting piece, which gives the measure of the skill with which Haydn knew how to test himself even in the quartet genre. Moreover, in the first half, after a few initial beats, the instruments stop, with an unusually long pause. The listener is going to ask himself: "What are they doing? Have they lost their mark?". Soon after, however, the instruments resume playing, as if nothing had happened.

Some tasty musical jokes are described by Leonard Bernstein, great conductor, analyzing the last movement of the *Symphony n. 102*. There is a first aria that looks like a dachshund puppy that comes out of the water and shakes off splashing on all sides. After a while that melody comes back, but secretly: Haydn makes it come out again when we don't expect it; and Bernstein defines it: "A sort of smaller brother hidden under the kitchen table". Later on, Haydn pretends to take back the melody, but then does not take it at all. And there are still other astonishing starts, with sudden "forte" and "piano".

Haydn composed as many as 107 symphonies. They are generally grouped into six periods, so called: Italian (1757-1760); baroque (1761-1765); pre-Romantic or Sturm und Drang (1766-1772); classic (1773-1784); French (1785-1789); English (1791-1795).

AN «ORDER» FROM CÁDIZ

Haydn also composed a lot of religious music, as it happened to Bach, Händel and many other composers. As is well known, the beauty of music has a deep relationship with the theme of the relationship between the human being and God. Haydn is Catholic: a Catholicism made of tradition, received automatically by the social context, in which the various religious institutions are an essential component of stability.

However, Haydn felt a "personal" adherence to the faith. In his correspondence there are phrases that document inner vibrations, whose authenticity there is no reason to doubt. For example: "When I think of God, my heart beats fast"; "In the morning I get up early. As soon as I get up, I kneel down to pray to God and Our Lady to help me even today "; "I never felt so pure as when I was engaged in *The Creation*" (*The Creation* is an oratorio which we will discuss later).

Even from the canons of the cathedral of Cádiz, a city projected on the Atlantic, in the western end of Europe, he received the "order", that is, the task of preparing a composition to be performed during Holy Week and having as its subject the seven words of Christ on the cross. As is well known, the Gospels report, overall, seven sentences pronounced by Christ while he was nailed to the cross. From those phrases Haydn took inspiration for a composition that bears, in fact, the title *The last seven words of the Redeemer on the cross*. This composition was written by him both in the quartet version and in the orchestral version.

I suggest listening to some of *The last seven words* in the quartet version (which is the most commonly performed and, perhaps, the most suggestive). As is known, the seven words (i.e. the seven sentences) are: «Father, forgive them because they do not know what they are doing»; «Today you will be with me in Paradise»; «Woman, here is your son; son, here is your mother »; «My God, my God, why have you forsaken me?»; «I am thirsty»; «Everything is done»; «Father, I place my spirit in your hands». Each of the sentences is commented on by a passage. The seven passages are preceded by a dramatic introduction and followed by the evocation of the earthquake which, according to the Gospel, occurred after Jesus' death. I particularly mention the phrases: «My God, my God, why have you forsaken me?» (where we find a cadence that evokes a dramatic question); «I am thirsty» (which begins with an invocation accompanied by pizzicato, and flows into a harrowing cry, masterfully rendered with the tension that arises from the combination of the most acute and the most serious registers); «Everything is accomplished» (where, despite the drama, we feel a sense of calmness, almost of relief, like someone who has concluded a great effort); «Today you will be with me in Paradise» (where there is an exquisite melody of dance that evokes Paradise, commonly represented by painters and poets as a garden in which the blessed dance in joy, accompanied by musical instruments played by angels).

DAD HAYDN

Haydn was very open to young musicians and very available to help. He gave lessons to both Mozart and Beethoven. If those lessons did not go on for a long time it was not for his bad will: it was because both Mozart and Beethoven had such strong personalities that they soon detached themselves from the master and took their own ways.

Haydn did not feel envies about those new stars. He did not save praises to Mozart, calling him "the greatest composer in the world" and rejecting the offer to direct the *Marriage of Figaro* and *Don Giovanni* because he did not consider himself capable of "measuring himself with such a prodigy". Mozart explicitly called him "dear dad".

With regard to Beethoven, Haydn had some difficulties. It was Haydn who invited him to Vienna when, passing through Bonn during a trip, he heard him play and he sensed his genius. But the character of Beethoven was, on the human level as on the artistic level, very different from Haydn's one and the mutual understanding lasted shortly. Beethoven took only a few lessons from Haydn; and the title of "Gran Mogol" which Haydn gave him (and which probably derives from the fact that Beethoven's face had an olive color, with traces of smallpox), remained famous.

Conversely, Haydn remained linked to Mozart though an affectionate friendship; he never failed to include his compositions in the concerts he directed; and, after the death of the great Salzburger, he pledged to spread his music so that the widow could derive some financial aid from it. And he wrote to the widow, Constance, promising that he would take care of one of the sons, teaching him composition concepts for free, "to replace his father at least a little." And the promise was kept.

BLOSSOMING OF «ELDERLY AGE»

In 1790 Prince Nicholas Esterházy died. The son, who happens to him, does not have the musical interests of his father; moreover, many things have changed since the beginning of the French Revolution, and the expenses of a palace have become enormous. The prince fires the orchestra. Even Haydn is fired, albeit with an annual pension and with the title of Kapellmeister.

The musician is looking for a new job. And luck favors him again. He meets a great entrepreneur of England, that deals with concerts and theatrical works. His name is Salomon and he is German, from Bonn: he proposes to Haydn - whose fame has come to England - to go to London to conduct and compose.

Haydn accepts and goes to London, leaving Vienna in December 1790 and then staying in the English capital until July 1792. There he composes symphonies (so called *Londoners*), conducts concerts (with his music and Mozart's), receives a degree to honorem at the University of Oxford, listens - with great emotion - to the *Messiah* of Händel, performed in the Westminster Abbey by an orchestra and one thousand performers choir. Haydn did not yet know Händel's music; in frony of this great performance, he cries of emotion and says of Händel: "He is the teacher of us all".

He gladly comes back from England enriched of successes. The London press writes: "We hope that the musical genius of our time deems it appropriate to establish his residence in England".

Haydn is now sixty years old. So he began his elderly age with an incredible blossoming of artistic production and international successes. In London he wrote six symphonies, which constitute the first group of *Londoners*. And he will go back to London in 1794, stopping there one more year, during which he will compose seven other symphonies (six of the second group of *Londoners* and the *Concertante symphony* n. 105).

Among the *London symphonies* (of which we have already "tasted" n. 100, n. 102 and n. 103), we can now choose n. 104, which is called *London* itself and is the last in the series of symphonies (it was composed in 1795). We can listen to the first half and once again taste the typical structure of the sonata form.

In his second stay in London, Haydn becomes passionate about horse racing, visits the Herschel telescope and is amazed by what he sees through it (the telescope theme will surface in the play *The World of the Moon*), he listen to much of Händel's music (who has spent most of his life in England and whose music is really loved by British people), he receives many and insistent solicitations to settle in England. British people are enthusiastic about his personality and his music: an enthusiasm that resembles what they have for Shakespeare. However, Haydn went back to Vienna in 1795 and resumed collaboration with the Esterházy, who reconstituted the orchestra. Two beautiful "oratorios" arise, influenced by Händel's music style: *The Seasons* and *The Creation*.

I will dedicate a specific paragraph to *The Creation*. Here we can listen to some pieces of *The Seasons*.

The oratorio *The Seasons* is, of course, divided into four parts, each of them dedicated to one of the seasons. It is a poem of rural life, wise and vigorous, centered on the voices of three soloists and animated by very wide interventions by the choir. The soloists are Simon, the mature and wise peasant (bass voice); Lukas, the young farmer in love (tenor voice); and Hanne, the gracious and virtuous daughter of Simon (soprano voice).

About *Spring*, I highlight the choir n. 2 ("Come, sweet spring") and the song of joy n. 8 (beautiful the stanzas: «Look at the earth, look at the water, look at the serene air ... Everything lives, everything vibrates, everything moves...»).

About *Summer*, I think is remarkable the recitative n. 10 of Lukas, which describes the dawn with words and music rich in mysterious vibrations, and, shortly thereafter, the trio and chorus n. 12, which evokes the sun's rising with a progressive rise of the voices and an explosion of the chorus at full volume; in addition, in

Summer we find the thunderstorm (n. 17) and the subsequent return of the stillness (n. 20), which evokes the ox, the quail, the cricket, the frog, with some excess of descriptivism that Haydn himself then had to criticize, defining it as «French rubbish».

About *Autumn*, I point out n. 29, with the cries of the hunters ("Tajò, tajò! Halàli, halàli!") on the suggestive and animated background of the horns and with the description of the hunt; n. 30, with the grape harvest and the hymn, overwhelming and dithyrambic, to wine («Olà, olà! Cheers to wine!»).

About *Winter*, we must remember the beginning (n. 32), with the description of the first mists (Andrea della Corte defined it "one of Haydn's sentimental peaks"); the song of the spinner at n. 38 ("Grumble, buzz, grumble! Buzz, little wheel, buzz!"); and the delicious «Lied with choir» n. 40, which I would call "the ballad of the girl and the knight" (it is the ridiculous tale of a knight who tries to buy a girl's love with gifts; the latter makes him walk away with a pretext, then she leaps on his horse and flees; the song is punctuated by interventions by the choir, which concludes with a laugh: "Ah! Ah! It serves him right!").

In this period also various masses are born, including the *Missa in tempore belli* (Mass in time of war): in fact, in 1796 the French invaded Austria. Haydn also composes the *Imperial Hymn*, in which he is influenced by the suggestions of the English national anthem *God save the king* and his enormous grip on English crowds. The haydnian hymn says: "Gott erhalte Franz den Kaiser" ("God save Francis the emperor"). The emperor Francesco II is very grateful and gives him a golden case with his portrait.

The theme of the *Imperial Hymn* is one of the themes of the Quartet op. 76 n. 3, which is also called, for this reason, *Quartet of the emperor*. On that theme the poet Hoffmann von Fallersleben wrote in 1841 the words of the official German anthem, in which the verse stands out: «Deutschland, Deutschland über alles» («Germany, Germany above all»); therefore the hymn will unfortunately become, in the following century, an expression typical of the imperialistic totalitarianism of Hitler (who, like me, lived his early youth during the Second World War can not forget the horrors evoked by that song: shooting, destruction of entire countries, deportations to Germany, gas chambers).

We can listen to the theme of the *Imperial Hymn* starting from the second movement (*Theme with Variations*) of the *Quartet op. 76 n. 3*. Speaking of quartets, I would point out that Haydn's quartets are an important aspect of Haydn's production. We have not dedicated space to them (nor would it be possible, given

98

the nature of this book). But it must be remembered that Haydn's quartet production had a notable influence on Mozart and Beethoven. Also, it may be interesting to listen to a passage from *Missa in tempore belli* which is also called Paukenmesse (*Mass of kettledrums*) because in it Haydn, given the characteristic of this mass, has made extensive use of kettledrums, instruments whose sound evokes noises of the battle.

THE BEST JOKE FOR A JOKER: ATTENDING HIS OWN FUNERAL

In 1805, the false news of Haydn's death spreads in Paris. The commiseration is intense and general. Funeral celebrations are organized immediately. Mozart's *Messa da Requiem* is performed in honor of the deceased. The great composer Cherubini composes a cantata for the occasion. The violinist Kreutzer composes a violin concerto on themes taken from the Haydn's oratorio *The Seasons*.

But Haydn is alive and well in Vienna. The misunderstanding is clarified and the pseudo-deceased comments amused: «What good people! I'm flattered by the honor they wanted me to do. I would have liked to direct my commemoration! ».

He is not dead, but it is very weakened. He is seventy-three years old, and it is a venerable age, one of which few were lucky enough to reach.

Haydn is worn down by his immense musical production, the result of a tireless and continuous activity. In 1808, at a solemn execution of the oratorio *The Creation*, Haydn is transported in a sedan chair, wrapped in shawls: he arrives in the theater to the sound of trumpets and kettledrums; the audience shouts "Viva Haydn!". The old master attends the execution of the first part, but then has to leave the theater to go back home, because of his weakness. He was probably suffering from arteriosclerosis; he also had a nasal polyp that, when it prevented him from breathing, required surgery.

On May 10th 1809 the French occupy the suburbs of Vienna. Napoleon installs himself in Schönbrunn in the splendid residence of the Habsburgs and on May 11th he bombs the city. On the 13th the city surrenders and the French occupy it. Napoleon, who is an admirer of Haydn, sets a guard service at his house because no one disturbs him.

The old master expired slowly and died on May 31st 1809. The news is not immediately released, and the funeral is, therefore, modest. Napoleon disposes however that a solemn funeral is to take place, with the performance of Mozart's *Requiem Mass*. Among those present at the solemn funeral is the French writer Stendhal, who later wrote a book entitled: *Vie de Haydn, Metastase and Mozart* (*Life of Haydn, Metastasio and Mozart*).

At this point, I would suggest to taste the exquisite second movement of the *Symphony n. 101*, called *The Clock*, which belongs to the group of symphonies composed in England during the last stay of Haydn. The evocation of the rhythm of the pendulum is one of Haydn's many musical games. The game is conducted here with effects of extraordinary formal elegance and intimate sweetness. The violins sing a sweet melody with the rhythmic accompaniment of the other instruments, among which dominate the flutes and bassoons, which mimic the regular ticking of the pendulum, symbol of the inexorable flowing of time. About the *London Symphonies*, the Italian Radio RAI Channel 3 offered its listeners a wonderful commentary by the musicologist Giovanni Bietti as part of the prestigious cycle of broadcasted lectures titled *Music Lessons*.

MUSICA E FELICITÀ

What in classical literature and the arts has been classicism, as a cult of beauty (inspired by models of Greek and Roman art), as the elaboration of fixed literary genres, as a rejection of all imbalance and contrast, as a triumph of enlightenment sense, in music it was above all Haydn's art.

His compositions are architectonically perfect musical constructions in the form, proportionate in their parts, sources of pleasure and aesthetic enjoyment, masterpieces of harmony. Normally imperturbable: a serene music that brings serenity; a music, in some way, objective, which reflects the graceful world of the eighteenth century, with its frivolities but also with its confidence in reason. A trust that is proper to the "Enlightenment Century" and which has the function of giving man security and happiness (a function that is now very much in crisis, in a world that doubts everything and has seen the myths of progress and unlimited development).

Not in vain, in what is called the "tonal palette" of Haydn, the major scales prevail sharply on the minor tones. The first are firm, bright, sunny. Unlike the latter, veined with melancholy and suffering, they have a laughing positivity and a fullness that inspire serenity, security and optimism.

In one of the last letters written by Haydn we read:

«Often, when I was struggling with obstacles of all kinds that opposed my work, an inner voice whispered to me: "There are so few happy and contented men here below that perhaps one day your work will be a source from which the men oppressed by anxieties and bent under the weight of life, will take a few moments of rest and relief". This was then a powerful incentive to persevere, the reason why I can now look back with deep satisfaction at what I have done in my life, through uninterrupted efforts and long-lasting commitment».

«Dad Haydn» is right: his music his music is still, even for the men of the twenty-first century, a source of joy, harmony, serenity, optimism.

LISTENING GUIDE TO A MASTERPIECE: THE CREATION

From England, where he had listened to many of Händel's oratorios, Haydn returned on his second voyage taking with him a "booklet" (a text to be played) in Vienna that a certain Thomas Lidley had drawn from Milton's *Lost Paradise*. He had this booklet translated into German, and on this German text he composed the oratorio *The Creation*.

The general structure of the oratorio follows the schema of the biblical narration of the creation of the universe, as described in the book of Genesis. It starts from chaos. Then God creates heaven and earth, the light, the firmament. Then the plant world and the animal world. Finally the man and the woman.

The narration faithfully follows the biblical text, punctuated occasionally by the phrase: "And God saw that it was good". The positivity and the goodness of creation, highlighted by the biblical text, are congenial to the character of Haydn, a character inclined to optimism, to smile, to serenity. The story is left to the voice of three angels: Gabriele (soprano voice), Uriele (tenor), Raffaele (bass). These three voices fulfill the task that is played by the evangelist in the *Passions* of Bach. However, the three angels are not limited to being unbiased narrators: they set in singing arias and recitatives that contain comments to the action of the creator, or express prayers, praises, invocations. Therefore they are interpreters of the feelings of the listener. This role, prayerful and contemplative, is also provided by the choir, in its frequent interventions.

The oratorio is divided into three parts: the first is dedicated to the creation of the physical and inanimate world (including vegetables); the second one is dedicated to the creation of the animated world (animals of all species and the human couple); the third part is dedicated to man and woman, to their relationship of reciprocal integration, to their relationship with God and the world. This third part no longer has the biblical text as a canvas: it is a free poetic invention in which Adam and Eve are interpreters aware of the praise that nature unconsciously makes to God following with faithful obedience the laws he has assigned. In this part, therefore, the voices of the angels are silent (with the exception of Uriele, who limits himself to open and close the same part with two short recitatives): the human couple is the leading actor, who seems to express with his preponderant presence the immense dignity of the human person, sung by the psalms and placed in main evidence in God's plan, which makes the human couple the pivot of creation and of the redemption plan. And it is this couple who turns to the various components of creation to invite them to praise God.

From a musical standpoint, the following passages seem to me worthy of particular note; the reader can, if he wants, listen to them in order:

N. 1: orchestral introduction that evokes primeval chaos. Haydn makes use of strong dissonances rather unusual at his times, so that this piece caused a certain scandal due to its harmonic boldness. But this technique of "harmonic obscuration" hosts a great descriptive efficacy. Also in n. 1 there is the beautiful moment of the creation of light: «And God said: "Let there be light". And the light was» («Und Gott sprach: "Es werde Licht." Und es ward Licht»). The passage is realized by the choir accompanied by the orchestra: the sounds are more and more muted, and at a certain point, with a beautiful effect, suddenly a dazzling sound of intense musical brightness explodes.

N. 21: the Raffaele's recitative, which describes the various species of animals. It is a very rich musical palette that often lingers, with taste, intelligence and moderation, on onomatopoeic sounds (that is, on sounds that imitate the voices and the sounds of nature). Giorgio Pestelli has wittily defined this part of the oratorio "a kind of encyclopaedia of natural-musical sciences".

N. 22: the wonderful Raffaele's theme, commenting on the creation of the animals. It ends with the words: «But the work is not yet completed. All this is missing a witness that manifests gratitude to God and knows to love, in him, his gifts ».

No. 24: Uriele's theme celebrating the creation of man. An unforgettable track for the sense of greatness and nobility that pervades it: the immense dignity of man is expresses with great effectiveness, celebrating his courage and strength, enhancing his intelligence and freedom, in which the image of the creator shines.

Massimo Mila said that this last piece sums up a century of Enlightenment thought. I believe the statement is correct and I fully agree with it. It seems to me that this can be complemented by this consideration: that Enlightenment thought here is to coincide impressively with the biblical conception, which springs from a modern interpretation without preconceptions. The present Christian theology sees in the Bible creationist conception a powerful boost towards the sdivinization of the world, towards the demythization of natural forces, towards the desacralization of institutions.

In contrast to many religions of the time, which deified the stars or animals or the forces of nature, the biblical vision affirms the "otherness" of the world with respect to God. "Creaturality" expresses, in fact, a differentness, not a identification, and therefore, while placing all the action of God at the origin, goes in the opposite direction to that sacralization. And this, in the biblical vision, is the first foundation of the secularity of the world and of human institutions. Not only that: giving life to creation as "other than oneself", God commits himself to respect the intrinsic laws of creation.

On the other hand, whoever keeps in mind the variety of "literary genres" can not confuse the poetic and symbolic language of biblical cosmogony with a scientific treatise: the literary genre used here by the Bible is a narrative genre, devoid of scientific claims, intended to be immediately understood by every man, belonging to any culture, and to transmit a message that focuses not on "how" but on "why" and has the essential concern to make clear the finiteness and contingency of creation and its otherness to God.

In this context the exaltation of man is common, albeit with different matrices, to the Enlightenment and to the biblical vision: the latter places man at the top of creation, makes him share - even in his "creaturality" - of the God's greatness, it even makes him a privileged interlocutor of God, a being with whom God establishes a personal relationship of love. All this is expressed perfectly in the theme of man's creation. Music becomes the vehicle of a positive and optimistic message: reading that message helps to appreciate the density, the ideal thickness of music.

Then, a moving episode of Haydn's life is linked to this theme. When Vienna was occupied by the Napoleonic troops, two French officers showed up at Haydn's house, when he was very sick. General fright, as happens in times of war and military occupation. But the two officers only wanted to pay tribute to the great master. They asked to be able to sing something in his presence. Haydn nodded. One of them sat at the piano, the other intoned the theme of man's creation. Haydn was moved. That "air" was becoming a sort of hymn of humanity: particularly significant in wartime.

In the Haydn's oratorio, the story of creation before the fall of man. Of this mysterious episode there is only an inkling, a disguised allusion, immediately dropped. It is in the last sentence of Uriele, who says: «Happy couple, happy forever, as long as you do not want to know one day a different happiness, you want to have everything and everything to know».

But it is not Haydn's optimistic nature to investigate the mystery of evil and sin. The choir that concludes the oratorio immediately takes over from Uriele, inviting earth and sky, men and worlds, to sing the glory of God and to praise the Lord for all eternity. On the other hand, the theme of creation did not involve, in itself, narrative dilatations to episodes subsequent to creation itself.

It seems to me, however, very significant that, in Uriele's sentence, the danger of a possible fall of the human couple is seen not in the realization of one's own humanity, nor in the use of one's own intelligence, nor in the exercise of sexuality (to sexuality, on the contrary, some pages are dedicated, where the love between man and woman expresses an image of God's love: Christ will then reveal that God himself is a community of persons and therefore love), but in anxiety to know everything and to possess everything: that is, in that unlimited faith in himself and in progress, which today reveals its intrinsic limits (the limits of development), and whose disastrous effects are breaking millennial ecological balances.

One last point: the choirs usually represent the most successful pieces of the whole composition with respect to recitatives and arias; in them, more than in the arias, all the vocal and instrumental teaching of Haydn is revealed.

The arias, on the other hand, are rather awkward, pompous, musically weak. Massimo Mila calls it "patriarchal and antiquated, comfortably predictable" music, which "rarely manages to rise to the sublime height of the subject". This judgment concerns only the arias, not the rest of the oratorio as a whole: which, on the contrary, presents the characteristics of a work of excellent quality, both in instrumental pieces and in choral pieces. Among the arias, then, the sublime is certainly drawn from the air of the creation of man, which we have referred to above as n. 24.

GETTING TO KNOW HAYDN

Haydn's symphonies numbering was made at the beginning of the twentieth century by the Austrian musicologist Mandyczewski. It is the traditional numbering, still widely used. A general catalog of all of Haydn's works (including, therefore, the symphonies) was then edited by Hoboken. In the coding convention of this catalog (today commonly adopted in the indication of Haydn's works), the work is preceded by the word Hob. (abbreviation of Hoboken). For example, the oratorio *The Creation* is referred to as Hob. XXI n. 2. But traditional numeration is still used to refer to the symphonies.

One of Haydn's oldest biographies was written by Abbot Carpani, who met him personally and collaborated with him: Giuseppe Carpani, *Le Haydine ovvero lettere sulla vita e le opere del celebre Maestro Giuseppe Haydn*, Silvestri, Milan 1812, republished in 1969 from Forni, Bologna. Another ancient biography is by Stendhal, *Vita di Haydn*, Passigli, Florence 1983.

More recent works are: Charles Rosen, The classic style: *Lo stile classico: Haydn, Mozart, Beethoven*, Feltrinelli, Milan 1982; Various authors, *Joseph Haydn*, in "L'Approdo musicale", Rai Eri, Turin 1960, n. 11; H. C. Robbins Landon and David Wyn Jones, *Haydn: vita e opere*, Rusconi, Milan 1988; Andrea Lanza and Enzo Restagno, *Haydn. Due ritratti e un diario*, EDT, Torino 2001 (contains *Note biografiche su Haydn*, by Georg August Griesinger and Albert Cristoph Dies, as well as a London Diary of Haydn).

Some interesting pages about Haydn, as well as about his symphonies and quartets are contained in the monumental *Storia della musica*, edited by the New Oxford History of Music, Feltrinelli / Garzanti, Milan 1991, vol. VII, pages 671-677 and 694-702.

On the religious sense of Haydn see also Rodolfo Venditti, *Ascoltare l'Assoluto*, third edition, Effatà, Cantalupa (TO) 2010, chapter 2, pages 56-63: *Onnipotenza di Dio e kenosis di Cristo nella musica di Haydn*.

An interesting analysis of Haydn's symphonies, preceded by a biographical profile, is in the book by Luigi Della Croce, *Le 107 sinfonie di Haydn*, EDA, Turin 1975.

On the influence that Haydn's music had in the chamber sector can be seen the essay by William Drabkin, *La musica da camera da Haydn alla fine dell'Ottocento*, in *Enciclopedia della musica*, directed by Jean-Jacques Nattiez, Einaudi, Torino 2001, vol. IV, pages 698-712.

WOLFGANG AMADEUS MOZART
(1756-1791)

Game and depth: two dimensions
of a complex and extraordinary musician

Posthumous portrait of Wolfgang Amadeus Mozart by Barbara Kraft, 1819.

The short life span of Mozart (thirty-five years) matches with a period that sees the transition from one era to another: the transition from the futile and powdered world of an aristocratic, immobile society, populated by powerful people and courtiers and in which the man in himself does not count anything, to a new world in which the French Revolution shakes the traditional authoritarian structures and Romanticism claims the autonomy and creativity of man himself, of his thought, of his art.

Mozart just comes to see the dawn of that new world (he will die, in fact, in 1791, two years after the Revolution). But the events of his life and the evolution of his music make us feel that passage: Mozart has accepted the changes that were taking place; he lived them, though not entirely consciously. And his music picked them up.

And this is how, on the one hand, we feel a burst of folksy moods in his work that break the patterns of a society founded on nobles and powerful people; and on the other hand we feel a music that is becoming more refined and "personalizing" more and more, up to taking on inflections that can be defined as "pre-romantic". What Haydn did not see during his long life, which began long before Mozart's birth and ended long after Mozart's death, he did in his brief but very intense human and artistic path.

This ductility of Mozart's art makes him very close and, in a certain sense, contemporary. In fact, even today, society is invested by profound transformations: the issue of human rights is emerging with particular strength, at the global level, which places man and the fundamental rights of which he is the bearer at the center of social and political life.

This "contemporaneity" of Mozart is one of the secrets of its relevance. Today, the diffusion of his music is very wide; concert halls and theaters in which his compositions are performed are always crowded; the enthusiasm for his music is intense and very high; theater, cinema, television, concert activities are interested in his life and spread his instrumental and theatrical compositions.

Wolfgang Amadeus Mozart was born in Salzburg, Austria, on the 27th January 1756. His father, Leopold, was a violinist at the court of the Prince Archbishop of Salzburg and initiated him to music from the early years of childhood. He was an authoritarian and interested man, who sensed his son's genius and wanted to plan a rational exploitation of it.

That plan included hours and hours of study of music, exercises on various instruments, attempts and rehearsals. Wolfgang quickly learned the harpsichord, violin, organ. At the age of five, he composed his first minuet. At six he gave his first concerts in Munich and Vienna, enjoying great admiration and great praise among his listeners. In Vienna the success was so resounding that it came to news to the Empress Maria Theresa of Hapsburg, who invited the Mozarts, father and son, to Schönbrunn (the beautiful summer residence of the Viennese court) and after the concert wanted to hold in her arms the little concert artist.

The exploitation of Wolfgang was sometimes done in ways that could be defined as "circus": the father, as if was exhibiting a trained monkey, was pleased to amaze the audience by letting the child play blindfolded, or with the keyboard of the harpsichord covered by a cloth, or by making him perform a song in which the right hand should play the highest notes, the left hand the lower notes, and an intermediate note should be played by pressing the corresponding key with the nose.

Wolfgang's little sister sometimes took part in the concerts: she was named Marianna, she was a few years older than him, and she was able to sing discreetly; together, Wolferl and Nannerl (these were their diminutives) formed a duet that increased public curiosity and success.

The mother, dominated by the paternal authority, as it was in that period, let this happen, even if it is conceivable that she suffered a bit while seeing the child forced to a so rigid discipline and kept far from the games and the entertainment of his peers. She was a cheerful, easy-going, humorous woman, who tried to lessen her husband's rigidity with her own lively and rough glee.

I would say that it is miraculous that little Mozart did not take to hate music, imposed in a way such massive and disproportionate to his age, and that his musical taste did not go irreparably bad in the circus performances he was forced to do. If he became the great musician we know, it is precisely because he had an innate inclination to music and artistic taste.

Of course, it is heartbreaking to look at the portraits of that time: the little Mozart appears with a wig and a sword, dressed in silk and lace, playing the harpsichord or being celebrated by gentlemen and ladies in wigs, dressed in silk and lace, in sumptuous and severe environments.

In that child's eyes is the nostalgia of running and playing games: a nostalgia that remained for his whole life and which constituted a dimension of his personality.

Basically, this child who, unlike the other children, had not been able to dedicate the years of childhood to play (spending them, instead in concerts, parties, court evenings together with adults), always maintained a child's mind and during all his life he vented his need for play by playing with the sounds. And, in fact, his music is a continuous and prodigious game with sounds.

Let's listen to Mozart's first works, composed at the age of five and six: the Minuet K 1 and the Minuet K 2. They are, of course, two elementary compositions, but graceful and pleasing.

An Always Travelling Boy

Between eight and ten years of age, little Mozart, always accompanied by his father, made triumphal journeys to Paris and London; in the following years he made three trips to Italy, going down to Naples and collecting successes: Milan, Bologna and Rome were the main stops.

Traveling was, at that time, a huge effort. It was done in horse-drawn carriages, in short stops (organized according to the change of horses), on rough and dusty roads, exposed to the elements, between risks of all kinds. There were, of course, neither trains nor paved roads; often staying in inns was precarious and uncomfortable; the carriages had no heating... The pain of traveling, added to the effort of the concerts, the commitment to study and preparation, the activity of the composer, certainly did not help the young Mozart's health and affected it, probably constituting a remote cause of his early death.

From this standpoint, the responsibility of the father seems to me serious, because of his relentless and systematic exploitation of the son's genius. Also from the psychological point of view, the strict dependence on his father damaged the boy and conditioned him for years, adding to the structure of his personality some traits of instability, indecision, childishness.

However, even from the detrimental situations, the solar nature of Mozart was able to take advantage: from that exhausting journey he knew how to derive great artistic advantages. He had very young contacts with some of the most influential figures in the European musical world: in London he met Johann Christian Bach, son of the great Johann Sebastian, and learned a lot from him, remaining then bound by a close friendship; in Milan he met Sammartini and Piccinni, two of the greatest Italian composers of that time; in Bologna he met Father Martini, one of the greatest music theorists, and received some lessons; in Rome he listened to the grandiose nine-voice *Miserere* of Allegri and with amazing self-confidence he rewrote it going by memory after coming back home, as the score of that piece was not public and only the performers knew it.

Of course, during those trips, Mozart also stayed in other Italian cities: in Rovereto, descending from the Brenner, he gave his first concert on Italian soil; in Venice he saw the famous Carnival, full of colors and music; in Turin he met the violinist Pugnani, who played at the court of the Savoy, met Paisiello, who was passing through that city, attended a play by Piccinni at the Teatro Regio and he played at Palazzo Barolo. And he treasured all these experiences.

He proved to be a great assimilator: like other musicians, he knew how to use all the musical experiences that he was gradually doing, but in a superlative way, and he knew how to translate them into life, stimulating the maturation of a very personal, extraordinarily rich, open and innovative art.

This prodigious ability to assimilate, exploited during his journeys in Europe, makes Mozart an authentically European musician.

During his journeys Mozart composed several theater pieces. From the period of travels in Italy (1769-1773), we can hear: the *Overture* of the play *Mitridate* K 87 (composed at fourteen); the *Overture* of the play *Ascanio in Alba* K 111 (composed at fifteen); the *Symphony K 130* (composed at sixteen). These are pieces that, even in the Haydian-type system, already reveal a certain originality. And again: the *Quartet K 20* (composed in Lodi); the *Quartet K 155* (composed in a hotel in Bolzano); the *Quartets K 156-160* (composed in Milan), and so on.

FROM SIGISMUND TO GERONIMO:
AN ABRUPT MANAGEMENT CHANGE

Meanwhile, Prince Archbishop Sigismund, an open man, an art lover and sympathetic towards the Mozarts, dies in Salzburg. He is succeeded by Geronimo di Colloredo, an authoritarian and unfriendly man with a bureaucratic spirit. He does not take kindly the journeys of the court musician Leopold Mozart and his son; those trips steal violinist Leopold from his Salzburg commitments. Therefore, he recalls him to the order and to the contractual commitments, establishing a new discipline and forbidding that the father accompany his son around the world.

And so when Wolfgang, obviously after his father's plans, will have to travel to Paris, the father will not be able to accompany him. Wolfgang is now twenty-one, but his father is too afraid that the young man, alone, can lose sight of the ambitious goals assigned to him; and arranges for the mother to leave with him.

It is 1777. At that time Mozart is a splendid composer of consumer music, that is, of fashionable music, targeted to entertainment: music dominated by 18th century grace, in which harmony is exquisite and imperturbable, in which there are no problems and there is only the search for a formal beauty that is an end in itself.

If we want to experiment two beautiful examples of this exquisite music, we can listen to the first movement of the *Concerto for violin and orchestra* K 219 and the first movement of the *Concerto for flute, harp and orchestra* K 299. The melodic vein and the formal perfection of these pieces, composed in that period, is admirable. If we want to push ourselves to the third movement of *Concerto K 219*, we will enjoy a lively *Rondò*, full of sparkling themes, with strong exotic components.

Mom, good and patient, leaves with Wolfgang. They make a stop in Mannheim, venue of a famous orchestra at that time. During his stay in Mannheim, Mozart falls in love with Aloysia Weber, one of the children of the Weber couple, with whom the two travelers have rented a room. Aloysia is an attractive and ambitious girl, with a good voice and aspiring to a concert and theater career.

This love brings Mozart to linger a bit in Mannheim: he is tempted to renounce to Paris, and makes plans for Vienna or Italy, where Aloysia Weber could have success with his voice. He writes to his father about that. But the father, who sees in this instability of his son the confirmation of the validity of his fears, responds with a very hard and intransigent letter, whose juice is "Aut Caesar aut nihil" (or Caesar, that is the king of France, or nothing, that is, going back home). Wolfgang resigns and obeys him: from Mannheim he leaves for Paris with the hope in his heart of being able, on his return, to cultivate his love for Aloysia and come to the wedding.

In Paris, Mozart's achievements are not amazing. This twenty-one is no longer a prodigy-child, and people do not recognize in him the child who had entranced the Parisian audience years before. Mozart is no longer a news, and his concerts do not receive the desired success. He gives some music lessons and also manages to have some "commissions": for example, the duke of Guines, who dabbles in flute and is the father of a girl who takes lessons of harp from Mozart, asks him to compose a concert for flute, harp and orchestra, that is a concert that offers the possibility to father and daughter to play together. Thus the *Concert for flute, harp and orchestra* K 299 was born, an exquisite masterpiece of entertaining music. And the piano *Sonata K 310* is also born, containing the famous *Turkish Marcia*, the result of the taste of that era for the so-called *turqueries* ("Turkish things") and a source of considerable success for the young composer. It still remains a pleasant and attractive piece, which denotes Mozart's fantasy and piano ability.

But the stay in Paris proves disastrous because of a tragic event that represents for Mozart the first experience of pain: the sudden death of the mother on July 3, 1778. This woman, who accompanied him with sacrifice, for maternal love and for obedience to an authoritarian husband, does not withstand the fatigue and discomfort of the long journey and the long period away from home.

In that foreign land the young Mozart lives an unspeakable drama. He remains alone, deprived of the comfort of his mother, among unknown people, in the impossibility of transporting the spoils to Salzburg with the responsibility of managing the news to be given to his father in the least traumatic way. With this goal, he writes a letter to him, telling him that his mother is not well; and at the same time he sends another letter to a priest, a family friend, Abbot Bullinger, revealing the atrocious reality and asking him to prepare Leopoldo for the tremendous news. Then, reassured by Bullinger, he writes to his father on July 9th, 1778, communicating the mournful news and trying to console him: he talks about his mother's peaceful death and expresses his faith in her otherworldly life and the hope of meeting her again one day. The three letters reveal aspects of the personality hitherto unknown: a surprising Christian wisdom, a mature acceptance of the tragic event, a sincere and profound faith in God, in his mercy, in his "will for good", beyond any contrasting appearance.

We can meditate with affectionate respect before this pain and relive the drama of Mozart listening to the second movement of a marvelous *Concerto for piano and orchestra* (K 488), which he will write much later (in 1786), but in which he vibrates a restrained pain and immense, together with the memory of a lost sweetness. It is an *Andante* of great beauty that directly touches the listener, "takes" him, makes him vibrate. Not by chance, the director Luigi Comencini used this piece as a soundtrack for the movie *Incompreso*, a film adaptation of the novel by the same name by Florence Montgomery, whose protagonist is a young boy whose mother died. On the other hand, if we want to listen to a piano piece composed in Paris at that time, we can listen to the piano *Sonata K 310*, with a strong dramatic impact.

The sad journey back to Salzburg, without the mother, is, at least, illuminated by the hope of meeting Aloysia in Mannheim, which is on the way back. Instead, in Mannheim Mozart has a nasty surprise: the Webers are gone; they moved to Munich because Aloysia made a career with her soprano voice.

Mozart runs to Monaco. There he finds the Webers, but he has another surprise, even harder: Aloysia has forgotten the young composer from Salzburg and is engaged to a singer whom she will marry soon; her ambitions have been easier to satisfy alongside an established singer than waiting for an obscure composer, a former prodigy-child.

The return to Salzburg is desolate. And it is mortifying because Mozart, returning empty-handed from Paris, finds himself in an embarrassing situation with the Prince Archbishop, with whom he had broken relations and to whom he begged to be allowed to resume his service at court, in the wake of his father.

But life in the provincial Salzburg is asphyxiated for a young musician who has made multiple international experiences. Mozart bites the brake; and it is a great relief for him when the Prince of Munich asks him to compose a work for the Munich Carnival of 1780. Prince Geronimo, by deference to the powerful colleague of Monaco, is forced to give permission; and so Mozart will stay for about six months in Munich, writing *Idomeneo*, a theater dramatic drama, whose music, crossed by flashes of tragedy, will have a great success in Munich.

Let's listen to the *Overture* of the *Idomeneo* K 366: a powerful and dramatic orchestral page that offers us a synthesis of the themes of the work.

In addition to the commitment of Munich, Mozart finds a way to escape from the Salzburg climate occasionally going to Augsburg, the Bavarian city from which his family comes and where an uncle of his lives who gladly hosts him. The daughter of that uncle is Tecla, a cousin who is a little older than him and quite naughty (the foul-mouthed letters that Wolfgang writes to her suggest a very free and unscrupulous relationship between the two).

AN HISTORICAL KICK IN THE ASS

In that same year (1780) the empress Maria Theresa, who for forty years reigned on the throne of the Habsburgs, died. His son Giuseppe II succeeds her. For the occasion, all the nobles of the empire convene in Vienna to pay homage to the deceased's body and to celebrate the new emperor.

Prince Geronimo of Colloredo also goes there, and there he is joined by Mozart. The latter is pleased to have the opportunity to return to Vienna, the animated capital of the empire. Less pleased he is when, after the celebrations, the prince goes back to Salzburg and orders Mozart to go back too. Mozart rebels against the order. The prince insults him. Mozart resigns and remains in Vienna. This is followed by a lively conversation between Mozart and Count Arco, administrator of the prince; the discussion becomes stormy because at that time the resignation of a worker had the flavor of an inadmissible injustice to the employer (as I said, Bach had even been arrested when he had resigned from the role conferred to him at the Weimar court) . The story will end with a forced farewell, with which Mozart will be kicked out of the court of Salzburg: and Count Arco will seal that expulsion with a very little aristocratic kick in the ass.

That kick became historical. It inaugurates, in some way, a new era, not only in the life of Mozart, but in the history of music. It is the sign of a real revolution. In fact, it closes the period in which Mozart was a court musician (i.e. a salaried official) and opens the period in which Mozart will work as a freelancer, as a free artist who lives on his own art. From now on, Mozart will no longer be obliged to compose on command of the master, to provide him with compositions of circumstance, consumer music. From now on, he will compose according to his own inspiration, writing music when and how his artist inspiration will suggest him.

It is 1781. The activity of free artist is not, for Mozart, a considered and deliberate choice, as it will be, soon, for Beethoven; it is the result of an instinctive impulse, of a "headshot" born from a disagreement that gradually became more pronounced and then precipitated into a self-dismissal, sanctioned by the kick of Count Arco. But this is anyway an absolute novelty in the history of music, a precursive novelty.

A «FREE ARTIST» AT WORK

Thus a period of fervent creative activity began. The *Haffner Symphony*, the concerts for piano and orchestra, the theatrical work *Il ratto dal serraglio* are born. Also the *Fantasia K 397* for piano is born. In my humble opinion, this *Fantasia* is an exceptional piece in which a real change of language is perceptible: it seems that Mozart abandons the classical style and experiences a new type of musical language, full of inner vibrations and jolts, of hesitations, of accelerations.

It is no longer about "consumer" or "entertainment" music: it is music-confession, in which the composer tries to express, through the notes, the feelings he has inside, without constructive concerns. It is the era of the *Sturm und Drang*, of pre-Romanticism. And Mozart's musical antennas capture the new cultural atmosphere: his music captures the ferments of Romanticism and sometimes it even seems to anticipate inflections and styles that will be typical of Chopin a half century later.

If we listen carefully to this *Fantasia*, we will immediately grasp this peculiarity. Moreover, we will be faced with a further surprise: in the composition two different languages coexist, juxtaposed. In fact, after a piano speech that is, as I said, of amazing news, towards the end the style changes and the *Fantasia* continues and ends in a typical eighteenth-century style.

Something is really moving in the music: a new way of conceiving its function is making its way. And Mozart is the preferred vehicle.

Of course, not all of Mozart's music is maintained at that height: there is also occasional music, pulled down quickly and certainly not exalted; but it does not obscure the best things.

Among these, there is the *Haffner Symphony* (so called because dedicated to the wealthy burgomaster of Salzburg, merchant and patron, awarded with the noble title): it is one of Mozart's major symphonies. The concerts, then, for piano and orchestra, all beautiful (we have already "tasted" the K 488), are one of the great artistic novelties: the piano was invented recently, quickly supplanting the harpsichord and fortepiano, and Mozart - great pianist, besides being a great composer - is the first to experiment with its sonority and to deal with that new instrument, destined to a brilliant affirmation.

I suggest to listen to a movement of the *Haffner Symphonie* K 385 (not to be confused with the *Haffner Serenade* K 250, also dedicated to the Haffner family): for example, the first movement. About *Concerts for piano and orchestra*, I propose to listen to the first movement of K 466, concert favored by Beethoven because rich in drama.

Il ratto dal serraglio is an exotic story in which Mozart tries for the first time to create a German musical theater: it is sung in German and built according to the popular form of the *Singspiel*, alternating sung pieces and spoken pieces. Its exotic setting (the "serraglio" is the harem of a sultan) also responds to the taste of the *turqueries* ("Turkish things"), which - as I said - was very fashionable at that time and of which we find the echo also in the *Rondò alla turca* that Mozart has included in the aforementioned *Sonata for piano* K 331.

You should also listen to this *Rondò alla turca*, as an interesting and emblematic example of that taste of the exotic, typical of the second half of the eighteenth century.

The theater opera has an important place in the Mozart production of this period. Mozart writes *The Marriage of Figaro* and *Don Giovanni*, two great masterpieces: the first from the famous comedy by De Beaumarchais (forbidden by the Habsburg censorship for antinobiliary allusions), the second centered on the legendary Spanish figure of Don Juan, the libertine who seeks only his own pleasure and that is ultimately tragically punished.

From *The Marriage of Figaro* (K 492), a very amusing and very musical masterpiece, I suggest to listen to the *Ouverture*, the theme of Figaro "Se vuol ballare, signor contino, il chitarrino le suonerò", the themes of the Countess Anna and of Susanna. Precisely in relation to this Mozart's opera, there are those who have highlighted how Mozart was the first musician who brought the unconscious to the scene and who was able to sculpt the temper of the individual characters through innovative music, completely unusual in eighteenth-century comic opera.

About *Don Giovanni*, it will be appropriate to listen at least to the *Overture*, rich in dramatic colors, the theme of Leporello "Madamina, il catalogo è questo", the duet "Là ci darem la mano", the serenade "Deh! Vieni alla finestra", the final scene with the ghost of the Commendatore and the chasm that swallows Don Giovanni. This work has been translated into a movie by the director Losey, with a transposition that respects Mozart's art and helps to taste it. Both works are on Italian text by Lorenzo da Ponte.

AN INTERIORIZATION PROCESS

Meanwhile, in 1782, Mozart married, against the will of his father, Costanza Weber, sister of Aloysia. It was a rather laborious decision, involving some "noosing" steps by the future mother-in-law:

a clever and interested woman, left widowed and worried about "arranging" three unmarried daughters, she had signed a written commitment to Mozart: to marry Costanza within three years, under penalty of a large fine. Costanza is a woman of mediocre standing, who will not understand her husband's genius; however, in some way she will be able to satisfy an elementary need of him: the need of a domestic reality, and the boyish need to play, to run, to joke in a crazy way, to fight with the cushions. Mozart will have six children and, with intimate drama, will have to watch the death of four of them.

In those years he will often find himself in financial difficulties, ill, without friends, lacking in success, badly accepted by the new emperor, without even his father (who died in 1787 and who, although terrible, was an important reference point for him), with a rather light and superficial wife, devoid of deep human depth, not unexceptionable in terms of fidelity. Substantially alone, melancholic, struggling with misery (also due to a foolish prodigality). In this situation, his music will become more and more impregnated with everyday life, will bring ever more frequent traces of his melancholy and of the progressive sadness: and even if it will continue to be an admirable sound architecture, full of jerk and joyful clarity, it will become gradually a mirror providing a more and more faithful image of his human life. Thus, it will undergo a process of interiorization, which will make it richer and deeper: however, as it moves away from the usual patterns, following other paths, it will be less and less understood by the public. And Mozart will also experience the pain of being abandoned by the public.

Of this intense interiorization we find significant indications, for example, in *Concerts for piano and orchestra* K 467 (second movement) and K 491 (first and second movement), in *Symphony K 550* (first movement) or in *Quintet for clarinet* K 581. *Symphony K 550* has an unmistakable vein of melancholy, underlined by the minor key; the *Quintet for clarinet* K 581 is characterized by melodies of extraordinary purity (the clarinet was an instrument particularly loved by Mozart, who also used it in one of his last concerts for solo instrument and orchestra: *Concert K622*). But all this does not eliminate the enchantment of joy, the impetus of a serenity never defeated and always full of childish amazement.

I quote as an example the famous *Little Serenade* (*Eine kleine Nachtmusik*) K 525, which is worth listening to, at least, the very famous attack of the first movement. In my opinion, also the quartet called *Delle dissonanze* can be placed within the framework of this process of internalization.

THE NEED OF FRIENDSHIP AND SOLIDARITY

These are the last years of Mozart's short life. His loneliness has become great. His nature inclined to cordiality and friendship suffers a lot. His need for support and help in the misery of poverty has become very acute. But that need finds it hard to find an adequate answer.

Mozart is Catholic; and not for simple tradition. His letters, and some of his religious compositions, reveal a deeply rooted and convinced faith, even if not always accompanied by behaviors coherent with it. I have often thought that Mozart would have found an environment suited to his expectations and aspirations if the believers of his time had lived the Gospel message fully and intensely: in that message lived fully, Mozart could have found an adequate response to his generosity and expansiveness, to his need for friendship and solidarity, to his vision about life (and in particular about music) as a daily miracle of beauty and love, a source of undying joy and image of God's infinite love.

Unfortunately, the times in which Mozart lived were times when the Catholic Church was strongly sclerotized and in which the Gospel (apart from some exceptional figures of saints) was scarcely practiced in its radical nature. The Church that Mozart knew was the politicized Church of the prince archbishop of Salzburg, strictly allied with nobles and powerful people, and being a power itself: very different from the Church of the origins or from the one of St. Francis of Assisi or of Pope John XXIII and Vatican Council II: although it must be remembered that Mozart found in a Catholic priest (Abbot Joseph Bullinger) an open hearted friend and confidant.

Therefore, in the life and music of Mozart there are moments of intense faith and authentic religiosity.

To enter that religious dimension there is a privileged «shortcut»: the very short passage *Ave verum* K 618, composed in the last year of life. It is an Eucharistic choral chant, with which the believer salutes and adores in the Eucharist the «true body of Christ, born of Mary, immolated on the cross for mankind». Paumgartner said that "in the narrow but immense space of its forty-seven bars, it is perhaps the highest masterpiece that Mozart has ever created." And Stinchelli said: "We are facing one of the most extraordinary examples of sacred music in all musical history, the fruit of an inspiration and concentration that leaves us astonished".

Let's listen to the complex but very sweet polyphony of this page. Its listening evokes to me a definition found in the *Mozartian Aphorisms* by Ferruccio Busoni: "His art (Mozart's) is similar to a sculptor's masterpiece: it is an image that is finished on every side".

Mozart tried to satisfy his immense need for solidarity and friendship by enrolling in Freemasonry, a secret association that was spreading in Austria (even Haydn had joined it) and that practiced mutual help among the members. It was considered, in the educated circles of the time, as a sign of "intellectual" distinction and of "humanistic" homologation that was not disdained even by high-ranking ecclesiastics. Moreover, the discipline of the arcane and the numerous symbols that Freemasonry used in its rituals struck Mozart's imagination and stimulated his poetic inspiration. He composed several "Masonic musics"; but above all, he was inspired by Freemasonry when he composed the theatrical opera *The Magic Flute*.

I propose to listen to some of the Masonic musics. For example, the *Funeral Music* K 477, written on the occasion of the funeral of two Masonic confreres, characterized by a deep emotion that suddenly lights up with a final chord in C major, almost a vivid light of hope. Or the *Small Masonic cantata* K 623.

FAIRY MAGIC, FOLKSY MOODS, REVOLUTIONARY FLAIRS: THE MOZART OF THE OPERA

The opportunity to compose *The Magic Flute* arose from a curious coincidence. Emanuel Schikaneder, a very peculiar theatrical manager, was working in Vienna. He ran a theater activity of popular type, oriented to strike people imagination, to entertain with the use of complicated and stunning theatrical machines, to impress with the magic and with the marvelous.

Schikaneder was also an actor and a director. Inspired by legends, stories and poems, he had created a fairytale and bizarre story, combining various successful ingredients: beasts and natural phenomena, exotic and mythical characters, the good, the bad and the wise, the love who wins with the help of magic (the magic flute played by Tamino), the evil that is defeated, the arcane ceremonies of the great priest Sarastro and his followers... The most prominent character was Papageno (name to be pronounced as in German, with a hard «g»: Papaghèno): strange figure of a bowler, dressed in feathers and always introduced by the sound of a pastoral instrument.

Schikaneder turned to Mozart to write the music for this opera. Mozart, attracted by the magical charm of the story and at the same time driven by the need to earn, accepted and set to work. A prodigious music came out, both in the variety of its inflections, and in the ability to capture the humors of people through the musical characterization of Papageno, having a temper of irrepressible vitality.

From *The Magic Flute* I propose to listen to the *Overture*, which is the synthesis of the themes of the work; the entrance of Papageno and its crackling and popular theme; the song of the Queen of the Night, an amazing piece in which the soprano's voice is bent to the most daring vocal acrobatics; the song of Tamino, interspersed with the sound of the magic flute; the hilarious duet between Papageno and Papagena; the solemn theme of Sarastro. Even the magic flute has had a wonderful film adaptation by the director Bergman: the vision of that movie makes a significant contribution to the full understanding of the work.

Although ill and close to death, Mozart wanted to personally direct the first performance of *The Magic Flute*.

It was a great success, repeated in many re-runs; and it is still a success, every time the play is performed (and it is frequently, given its popularity and its everlasting modernity).

A more subtle ability to grasp and enhance folksy moods and practices, and to feel their gradual imposition in a social life still marked by the customs of the ruling class, was already identifiable in *Don Giovanni*, a work also belonging to the maturity of Mozart. The *Don Giovanni*, that I already mentioned, has been read in a plurality of keys, including the psychoanalytic one which tends to see the relationship between Mozart and his father in the relationship between Don Giovanni and the Commendatore.

But there is also the key to revolutionary intuitions: in the complex structure of the famous *Minuetto* that delightfully appears in the first act of the work, Roman Vlad saw the imminent emergence of the subaltern classes, noting how in the aristocratic dance of the *Minuet* Mozart has inserted a *Contradanza*, that is a typically popolar dance (that *contra* is the literal transcription of the English term *country*). I said «imminent» because *Don Giovanni* was first performed in Prague in 1787, that is two years before the outbreak of the French Revolution.

Let's listen to the *Minuet* of the first act of *Don Giovanni*, paying attention to the introduction of the *Contradanza* in the structure of the minuet.

A REQUIEM COMPOSED FOR HIS OWN DEATH

While composing *The Magic Flute*, Mozart receives a strange visit, which disturbs him. At his door is a gentleman dressed in black, who does not reveal his name and sais to have been sent by a client who wants to remain unknown. The stranger instructs him to compose a Requiem Mass, promising him a generous reward, giving him a substantial deposit and telling him that he will return after a while to collect the completed work. Mozart remains upset. He is very sick. The mysterious figure, the strange circumstances of the "commission", the object of the assignment (the Requiem Mass is a Mass for the dead) give him the impression that that character is a messenger of death, come to give him a mysterious warning so that he can prepare to die.

He gets busy at work, interrupting the drafting of *The Magic Flute*. The unknown person returns more than once to control the progress of the composition. Mozart has not finished it yet, because he has returned to devote himself to *The Magic Flute*. Now he resumes the Mass, but his health gets worse quickly. He will not be able to finish it. It will remain unfinished and will then be completed, on the basis of notes left by him, by his pupil Süssmayer.

The strange episode of the unknown messenger gave rise to legends. One of them has been included in the movie *Amadeus*, in which the director Milos Forman, following the traces of a drama by Shaffer, in turn resumed in a microdrama by Pushkin, has credited the hypothesis that the guise of the unknown messenger was hiding Antonio Salieri, composer contemporary of Mozart and official musician at the court of Vienna; the legend sais that Salieri, envious of the great Mozart's art, with that stratagem wanted to take possession of the composition and make it his own.

This hypothesis, exacerbated by the fact that, in the movie, Salieri is presented as the one who assists Mozart in the last days of life and who writes the notes of the Requiem Mass under his dictation, is profoundly anti-historical, as it is the legend - the result of gossip, then collected by Pushkin to obtain the short drama *Mozart and Salieri* - according to which the envy of Salieri would have come to the point of eliminating the rival by causing his death with poison.

In reality, no element supports such a hypothesis. According to another hypothesis, recently advanced, death would have been caused by the beatings of a husband (certainly Hofdemel) whose wife was a pupil of Mozart and would have been courted by him. The question of Mozart's death is much debated, and this is not the place to discuss it. However, it should not be forgotten that Mozart was seriously ill, of a disease that doctors then diagnosed as acute miliary fever (a kind of tuberculosis) and that some people believe to have been a form of nephritis.

According to Norbert Elias, he was in extreme need of feeling loved, and would surrender to death when, in his loneliness, he experienced a radical loss of meaning in his life. As for the mysterious messenger, it was clarified that he was an envoy of a certain baron Franz von Walsegg, who delighted in composition, held an orchestra at his disposal in the castle of Stuppach and used the "commission" system through an unknown messenger to buy compositions of important authors and make them pass as his own: having died his wife, he had adopted the same system to get a Requiem Mass written by Mozart and to have it run as his own on the anniversary of her death.

I will soon dedicate a special paragraph to the *Requiem*. I propose here to listen to some of the last pages of Mozart. I suggest the *Concert for clarinet and orchestra* K 622: we listen to the wonderful melody of the second movement; in it the clarinet sings with its full and pasty voice, rich in suggestion. The melody was written between September and November 1791, that is during the last months of Mozart's life. The whole concert is characterized by the prevalence of the clarinet timbre, which Mozart employs with great mastery the various registers, alternating them with great variety, so that the rapid alternation of sharp sounds and serious sounds gives the singular impression that the instrument dialogues with himself.

A SHABBY FUNERAL AND A MASS GRAVE

Mozart died on December 5th, 1791. He left the *Requiem* interrupted in the part of *Dies irae*, to the stanza *Lacrymosa dies illa.*

His wife, a sister-in-law and the pupil Süssmayer were beside him. On the day of the funeral, Vienna was in very bad weather. No one accompanied the hearse to the cemetery: the wife was cool and for this reason she gave up the accompaniment. The body of Mozart was thrown into a mass grave, without anyone taking care to put a distinctive sign that allowed the tracing and identification.

It was no longer possible to identify the point where Mozart had been buried and recover the body to give it a proper burial. In Vienna, Salzburg and other cities there are monuments that honor Mozart. But a tomb does not exist, where men can honor the spoils of one of the greatest musicians in history.

As it was the custom of the time, on his deathbed they did a plaster cast of his face, the so-called "death mask". That plaster cast fell and broke after some time. Costanza swept away the pieces: it did not seem worthwhile to put them back together, so that the true imprint of her husband's physiognomy remained to posterity.

Three years earlier Mozart wrote his greatest symphony, called *Jupiter* (that is Jupiter, the father of the gods, according to classical mythology) for its grandeur. I propose to listen to the last movement of this symphony, which contains a fugue that resembles Bach's rigor and monumentality.

MOZART OR AMADEUS?

Mozart's personality is apparently simple and linear, but it's very complex, indeed. We have already had occasion to mention it.

A mixture of childishness and maturity, of limpid joyousness and of dramatic tension, of vulgarity and purity, of refined art and of pedestrian craft, of proud autonomy and of supine acceptance of paternal direction.

His letters, which make up a wide epistolary, reveal very noble impulses next to unexpected scurrilties: a symptom of immaturity that had not resolved some fundamental nodes of the person development. And the fact that Mozart was, for many human aspects, an immature is confirmed by the type of relationship he had with his father and, perhaps, by the way he set up and led his relationships with his wife.

However, for sure Mozart was not the vanished and almost stupid guy who presented us in the film *Amadeus*: a movie that, if from a spectacular point of view can be said to be successful (I remember, for example, the extraordinary vivacity with which is depicted the popular theater of Schikaneder) and if from the musical point of view has the advantage of offering a soundtrack very rich in Mozart music, from the standpoint of human and artistic substance of the protagonist seems to me very far from the reality that can be obtained from the existing biographical material. It is worth mentioning the textual words with which Enrico Stinchelli defines the Mozart presented by the film: «A superficial and stolid Mozart... a naughty boy with horse laugh who writes wonderful music... a brilliant idiot killed by the dark Salieri...». And Giorgio Pestelli rightly reinforce the message, pointing out that the protagonist of the film (actor Tom Hulce) would have claimed to have been inspired by the temper of John McEnroe, a "tennis genius who quarreled with everyone", then an "image of transgression within a conservative vision": while Mozart - Pestelli says – was «the opposite of this: he was someone who changed everything in the music of his time without destroying anything».

Through the times, Mozart's music has experienced different phases and alternating fortunes. For a long time it was appreciated only as an expression of eighteenth-century grace: it was considered, in essence, as the highest and most refined product of that style that had given rise to the music of Haydn and many other composers of the eighteenth century.

It was the thesis of the "Apollonian Mozart", that is of the Mozart absolute interpreter of an ideal of beauty and grace: the triumph of harmony and classical form. The adjective "Apollonian" (from "Apollo", one of the gods of classical mythology) was, in fact, given to a sculpture or a painting that reproduced with absolute perfection the beauty of the human body and the harmonious proportion of its forms. And it is significant that Mozart's music has frequently been compared to the art of Raphael, supreme expression of beauty and classic balance.

But then the so-called demonic of Mozart was discovered; demonic not in the sense of "infernal", but in the sense of "genius", of passion, of torment, of drama (from the Greek word *dàimon*, meaning "genius"). And then came the other side of the moon, the other dimension of Mozart: the one we tried to highlight by following the path of his life and his work.

It is a dimension that presents a singular expressive mobility, that is a capacity to range over, in a single passage, from one expressive register to another, from one feeling to another, with sometimes imperceptible passages that mark a development of affections: it is the so-called «broken affect technique» brought to light by the musicologist Hermann Abert.

All in the name of that sublime unconsciousness that characterizes the art of Mozart: according to Massimo Mila, such unawareness keeps Mozart "on this side" of Romanticism (of which, however, he knows how to grasp - as we have seen - the first ferments) and it is the secret of its purity.

LISTENING GUIDE TO A MASTERPIECE: IL REQUIEM K 626

I chose this composition because it is the last great masterpiece of Mozart and because, given the Latin text and the particular liturgical structure, it requires a "decoding" to be fully enjoyed.

As I have already said, the *Requiem* is a Mass for the dead. As is known, according to the Catholic faith, the Mass (today more frequently called "Eucharist": from the Greek *eukaristéo*, which means "thank") is the "Supper", instituted by Jesus in the cenacle in the evening before his death on the cross. In that dinner, breaking bread and offering wine to his friends, Jesus said: "Take and eat: this is my body. Take and drink: this is my blood. Do this in memory of me".

According to the Catholic faith, the words of Christ refer to a real presence of him in bread and wine: real presence that he announced when, after the multiplication of the loaves, he said that his body and his blood were really food and drink, and with this statement aroused scandal and caused the departure of many people (John 6, 22-71). Just as the Passover was the memorial of the passage of the Red Sea and therefore of the liberation of the people from the slavery in Egypt, so the Mass is memorial of the Passover of Jesus, that is of his passage from the death

127

(occurred in the sacrifice of the cross) to the resurrection: a passage destined to involve all men in a project of liberation from evil and salvation in love.

As a "sign" of this memorial Jesus chooses the convivial moment, that is, the most typical moment of friendship and sharing. The believer thus relives, as a community, the death and resurrection of his Lord, puts himself in direct contact with him (through that extraordinary "invention" of the love of God which is the Eucharistic presence), and through him he addresses to the Father, expressing his own adoration, his thanks, his need for conversion, his own prayer.

Among the possible purposes of prayer is suffrage for the dead, so that the Lord forgive their faults and their sins and welcome them in the joy of his home, where love and fraternity reign (according to the revelation of Jesus, the essence of God is precisely love, that is, the reality to which man aspires from the depths of his own being).

To understand Mozart's *Requiem* it is essential to have an idea of the structure of the Mass.

This is the general structure of the Mass. It begins with an entrance prayer, once called *Introito*, followed by the request for forgiveness (*Kyrie eleison*, "Lord, have mercy") and the *Gloria*. Then the readings of passages from the Bible follow and, above all, from the Gospel. After reading and meditating on the Gospel, the assembly of believers recites the *Creed*. After this "liturgy of the Word", the true "Eucharistic liturgy" begins: the celebrant priest offers to God, in the name of the whole community of believers, the bread and wine that will soon be consecrated: this act is called *Offertory* and consists of some prayers and offer gestures. Then the priest intones the *Preface*, a hymn of thanksgiving that ends with the *Sanctus* ("Holy, Holy, Holy is the Lord, God of the universe"). It follows the consecration of bread and wine, in which the priest repeats the gestures that Jesus made and the words he spoke at the last supper: "Take and eat, this is my body... Take and drink, this is the cup of my blood, poured out for you...". After the consecration the *Benedictus* is sung ("Blessed is he who comes in the name of the Lord"), which is a passionate greeting to him who has made himself present under the species of bread and wine. Then there are some prayers that the community addresses to God through Christ present on the altar. This is the moment of *Communio*, that is, of "Take and eat": the faithful, after invoking the *Agnus Dei qui tollis peccata mundi* ("Lamb of God, take the sins of the world upon you, have mercy on us; give us peace "), receive the body of the Lord, while the prayer of the *Communio* is recited (or sung). The Mass closes with the blessing, with which every member of the faithful is invited to go into the world, bearing witness to the love of Christ with coherence and fidelity.

On this fundamental structure of "Eucharistic supper", Mass for the dead presents some particularities. *Introit, Offertorio* and *Communio* are prayers intoned to the suffrage of the dead. The *Agnus Dei* presents a variant: it invokes *Dona eis requiem* ("Give them peace"). Instead of the *Gloria* and the *Creed* a "sequence" (i.e. a particular poetic text) is read, entitled *Dies irae* and dedicated to the problem of the afterlife and of the universal judgment. It is a medieval poem, which bears all the limits of the Middle Ages, since it gives much space to a vision of God as a judge punishing blame, rather than as a loving father who forgives the repentant prodigal son and welcomes him back to his home. However, it is a literary poem very beautiful, which, while presenting God as a terrible judge, does not neglect to highlight his mercy.

At the time of Mozart the mass was celebrated in Latin (as it was until the Vatican Council II) and therefore the texts put in music by Mozart are in Latin. It is very useful to follow the execution having in front of the Latin text (to grasp and follow the progress of the song), and at the same time its translation (to understand the meaning of the words that are sung and therefore better penetrate the beauty and meaning of the music).

INTROIT. The text reads: «Requiem aeternam dona eis, Domine; et lux perpetua luceat eis» («Oh Lord, give them eternal rest and perpetual light may shine for them»). This phrase is sung by the choir with an intense and heartfelt invocation: the song is almost whispered, like someone who is afraid of waking up a person who rests. Immediately afterwards, the soprano goes on to say: «Te decet hymnus, Deus, in Sion, et tibi reddetur votum in Jerusalem» («To you befitting, oh God, the hymn on Mount Zion, to you are given thanks in Jerusalem»); and then the chorus resumes singing: «Exaudi orationem meam, ad te omnis caro veniet» («Fulfill my prayer: to you every being will come»).

KIRIE ELEISON. This supplication of piety unfolds through three invocations: «Kyrie eleison» («Lord, have mercy»); «Christe eleison» («Christ, have mercy»); «Kyrie eleison» («Lord, have mercy"). Mozart has set this part of the mass in the style of the fugato: the three invocations are a wonderful escape, begun by the male voices of the choir, continued (with «Christe eleison») by female voices, and concluded jointly by the whole chorus with the accompaniment of strong kettledrum shots.

DIES IRAE. It constitutes the largest part of this mass. As I have already had occasion to say, Mozart died during the composition of this passage: exactly in the stanza *Lacrymosa dies illa.* His pupil Süssmayer then continued and concluded the mass, completing also some passages in which Mozart had left incompleteness. We therefore follow, step by step, this poetic text, to verify the musical "translation" of Mozart:

1) *Dies irae, dies illa / Solvet saeculum in favilla: / Teste David cum Sybilla.*
The day of wrath will be one in which the world (the "century") will be destroyed in the flames, as predicted by David and the Sibyl (that is, from the Bible and also from the pagan religions).

This attack is grandiose, we could say apocalyptic: the music, in the power of the chorus and the orchestra, shows the majesty and the terror of God, supreme judge. And to underline the universality of the judgment the text cites David (that is, the biblical prophecies) and the Sibyl (that is, the pagan predictions).

Quantus tremor est futurus / Quando judex est venturus / Cuncta stricte discussurus!
How much fear there will be, when the judge will severely judge everything!

Precisely to the judgment of God this verse refers; the music dilates it, immediately repeating the first verse and intertwining the two verses in an overwhelming crescendo.

2) And here, after a moment of silence, the *Tuba mirum*, which opens the second episode.

Tuba mirum spargens sonum / Per sepulchra regionum / Coget omnes ante thronum.
The trumpet, spreading a wonderful sound among the sepulchers of every part of the world, will gather everyone before the throne of God.

The verse is intoned by the trombone, which evokes the trumpet of universal judgment. The trombone immediately takes over a stupendous bass voice, which continues the chant of the verse with the extremely suggestive accompaniment of the trombone itself. But the episode consists of five strophes that follow each other with a very close connection, singing the victory over death, the resurrection of the bodies, the appearance of the supreme judge, the great book that he will open, the fear that will invade all those present, who will look around for someone who can effectively defend them.

The Latin verses say this with great power of synthesis:

Mors stupebit, et natura / Cum resurget creatura / Judicanti responsura.
Liber scriptus proferetur / In quo totum continetur / Unde mundus judicetur.

Judex ergo cum sedebit / Quidquid latet apparebit: / Nil inultum remanebit.
Quid sum miser tum dicturus? / Quem patronum rogaturus / Cum vix justus sit securus?
Death and nature will remain astonished when every creature rises again to respond to the one who judges it. A written book will be brought forward, which contains everything that will be the object of judgment. Then, when the judge sits down, all that is hidden will appear: nothing will go unpunished. What will I say, then, I miserable? Whom will I call as a defender, since the right man will barely be safe?

Mozart uses a very effective and expressive expedient. Started, in the first stanza, with the bass voice (a deep voice that seems to evoke the opening of the tombs), continues with the other strings entrusting them gradually to increasingly sharp registers, in a scalar progression that gradually increases the tension of the piece. So, after the bass, here is the voice of the tenor exploding, which with that *Mors stupebit* seems to visually express the surprise of the exceptional event that defeats death. After the tenor, the contralto sings: «Judex ergo»; and then immediately afterwards, without pauses, the soprano takes over, singing «Quid sum miser». The other three soloists are associated with the soprano in repeating this last stanza.

3) Here is the third episode of the *Dies irae*.

Rex tremendae majestatis / Qui salvandos salvas gratis / Salva me, fons pietatis.
King of tremendous majesty, who saves for free those who are to be saved, save me too, oh source of mercy.

The word *Rex* is like a mallet blow, repeated three times on its own, and then a fourth time with the rest of the sentence. On those hammer blows, sung by the whole choir, the invocation *Salva me* flourishes, sung by the female voices and then repeated by the male voices, like a prayer that rises from the depths of the soul. The chiaroscuro created by the stark contrast between the powerful blows of the Rex and the tenuous, passionate cry of the *Salva me* is a very effective and expressive solution. The episode closes with the *Rex tremendae majestatis*, strongly marked by the chorus as a whole.

4) The fourth episode is the *Recordare*. It is perhaps the longest episode. It consists of seven verses and is entirely dedicated to the theme of God's mercy and to the invocation of the faithful. The humanity of Jesus appears to you as the «bridge» between man's misery and the unattainable greatness of God (Jesus is defined as «pontiff», which literally means «bridging factor», builder of mediation).
Here are the stanzas:

Recordare, Jesu pie, / Quod sum causa tuae viae: / Ne me perdas illa die.
Quaerens me, sedisti lassus, / Redemisti crucem passus: / Tantus labor non sit cassus.

Juste judex ultionis, / Donum fac remissionis / Ante diem rationis.
Ingemisco tamquam reus, / Culpa rubet vultus meus: / Supplicanti parce, Deus.
Qui Mariam absolvisti / Et latronem exaudisti / Mihi quoque spem dedisti.
Preces meae non sunt dignae, / Sed tu bonus fac benigne / Ne perenni cremer igne.
Inter oves locum presta / Et ab hoedis me sequestra, / Statuens in parte dextra.
Remember, oh compassionate Jesus, that I was the cause of your man's journey: make me not be lost on that day. Looking for me, you sat tired, you redeemed me suffering on the cross: so much effort is not useless! Fair judge that punishes, give me the gift of your forgiveness before the day of judgment. I moan as guilty, my face blushes with guilt; forgive, oh God, who begs you. You, who absolved Mary Magdalene and granted the good thief, gave hope to me too. My prayers are not worthy of listening, but you, who are good, benignly make sure that I am not burned in eternal fire. Give me a place among the lambs and distinguish me from the goats, placing me on your right.

This episode begins with the sound of cellos, to which are added immediately the horns, and then the entire orchestra. Then the soloists enter, who sing with a dense interweaving of voices, much worked especially in the *Ne me perdas*. *Quaerens me* is sung by the bass, *Redemisti* by the soprano, with an evocative juxtaposition of extreme registers. *Juste judex* is an intense invocation that continues with the *Ingemisco*: beautiful, in the latter, the accompaniment of the orchestra, which develops in crescendo up to the *Supplicanti*. Tender invocation of the *Qui Mariam absolvisti*: already the text is permeated with delicate poetry (the believer reminds his Lord of the gestures of mercy performed by Jesus and invokes them as a reason for obtaining forgiveness); the music, then, covers it with very sweet notes. The *Preces meae* is again a dense interweaving of pleading voices, which results in a cry to the *Ne perenni cremer igne*. Very nice also *Inter oves*, sung by the bass, to which the other solo voices are associated, that conclude the episode.

5) The fifth episode is the *Confutatis*. The terribleness of the *Rex tremendae majestatis* reappears. But immediately, in contrast to that thundering reason, the *Voca me cum benedictis* makes its way, which is like a light angelic song that comes from astral distances and that tempers the bitterness of *Confutatis*.

Confutatis maledictis / Flammis acribus addictis / Voca me cum benedictis.
Oro supplex et acclinis / Cor contritum quasi cinis / Gere curam mei finis.
Judged and condemned the accursed and thrown into burning flames, call me with your chosen ones. Please, suppliant and prostrate, with a repentant heart, as in ashes, take care of my destiny.

This second stanza of the episode is very expressive: the music follows, with the voices, a descending drawing, as if to bow deeply, to prostrate itself on the ground; and the orchestral accompaniment is intense and throbbing, following step by step the touches of feelings.

132

6) Finally, the sixth episode.

Lacrymosa dies illa / Qua resurget ex favilla / Judicandus homo reus.
Huic ergo parce, Deus, / Pie Jesu Domine, Dona eis requiem. Amen.
It will be a day of weeping in which the guilty man will rise from the fire to be judged. To this man, therefore, forgive, oh God, oh merciful Lord Jesus, give them rest. Amen.

Mozart wrote only eight bars of this episode. Before the beginning there is a singular isolated note: a chord preceded and followed by a pause; constitutes an element of transition between the end of the fifth episode and the beginning of the sixth. After this connection, a soft and throbbing motif begins with the violins: it is a sobbing design on which the chorus is immediately introduced singing the *Lacrymosa*. These are just a few bars, but they are enough to give the measure of Mozart's art. On the track of that cue, Süssmayer continued. But I would say that the diversity of hands is very clear: the continuation lacks the initial momentum, has something static and tiring, very different from the spontaneity of the beginning. Everything closes with a choral *Amen*.
Let's try to listen to the *Lacrymosa* trying to catch the moment of the change of hands; it is on these notes - we may well say - that the heart of Mozart ceased to beat: just as he invoked the mercy of the Lord.

OFFERTORIO. The first episode is partially by Mozart, whose words are as follows:
Domine Jesu Christe, Rex gloriae, libera animas omnium fidelium defunctorum de poenis inferni et de profundo lacu... Sed signifer sanctus Michael repraesentet eas in lucem sanctam, quam olim Abrahae promisisti et semini eius.
Lord Jesus Christ, King of glory, free the souls of all the faithful departed from the pains of hell and from the deep abyss... But the holy archangel Michael will bring them to the holy light, which you promised to Abraham and his descendants.

Beautiful, in this episode, the *Quam olim Abrahae*. It is a fugato of great effect and significance: the choral singing expands in ever more distant waves, offering the musical image of the succession of generations left by Abraham, father in the faith. We remember that Abraham was childless and had faith in God who, against all evidence, promised him a numerous lineage like the stars of the sky and like the grains of the sand of the sea. The music gives us, with its fugato, the image of this historical dimension: from the word «Abraham» the generations that are spreading from century to century seem to come out, forming an immense people, in successive and inexhaustible waves.
And the insistent hammering of the chorus on the word *promisisti* seems to want to remind the Lord of his promise and ask him to keep it.

The *Offertorio* is followed by: the *Sanctus* (with abundant use of kettledrums), the *Benedictus* (sung by the soloist voices, which flow, then, in a fugato) and the *Agnus Dei*, all composed by Süssmayer. Amongst them, the most original appears to be the *Agnus Dei*, for certain shivering and suggestive passages and for others harmonically successful.

The *Requiem* closes with the *Communio*, which incorporates, both in words and in music, ideas and themes of the *Introit*.

GETTING TO KNOW MOZART

The numbering of Mozart's works is always preceded by the letter K: this letter is the initial of the word Köchel, which is the surname of the person who compiled the most widespread and authoritative catalog of Mozart's works. Sometimes it is written KV, instead of K: KV are the initials of the words *Köchel Verzeichnis* (Köchel's Catalog).

To learn about the life and art of Mozart I was helped by reading a short essay by Massimo Mila, *Wolfgang Amadeus Mozart*, published by Edizioni Arione, Turin, in 1945 (later reissued in 1980 by Studio Tesi, Pordenone). In addition, the books by Ludwig Ferdinand Schiedermair, *Mozart*, Garzanti, Milan 1942, and Wolfgang Hildesheimer, *Mozart*, Sansoni, Florence 1977 (edited again by Rizzoli, Milan 1994) were very useful to me.

The bibliography on Mozart is very rich (I refer especially to the Italian or translated into Italian books). I remember, in chronological order of publication: Alfred Einstein, *Mozart: il carattere e l'opera*, Ricordi, Milano 1951; Camille Bellaigue, *Mozart: vita e arte*, Rizzoli, Milano 1955; Aloys Greither, *Mozart*, Einaudi, Torino 1962; Beniamino Dal Fabbro, *Mozart*, Feltrinelli, Milano 1975; Bernhard Paumgartner, *Mozart*, Einaudi, Torino 1978; Eduardo Rescigno, *Mozart*, Fabbri, Milano 1979; Karl Barth, *Wolfgang Amadeus Mozart*, Queriniana, Brescia 1980; Florian Langegger, *Mozart padre e figlio*, Mondadori, Milano 1982; Enrico Stinchelli, Mozart: la vita e l'opera, Newton Compton, Roma 1986; Gernot Gruber, *La fortuna di Mozart*, Einaudi, Torino 1987; Stanley Sadie, Mozart, Ricordi/Giunti, Milano 1987; Philippe Autexier, *Mozart*, Champion, Paris 1987; Robbins Landon, *Mozart. Gli anni d'oro (1781-1791)*, Garzanti, Milano 1989; Idem, *L'ultimo anno di Mozart: 1791*, Garzanti, Milano 1989; Danilo

Faravelli, *Wolfgang A. Mozart, un musicista fra Antico Regime e Mondo Nuovo*, Editori Riuniti, Roma 1989; Giovanni Carli Ballola e Roberto Parenti, *Mozart*, Rusconi, Milano 1990; Franco Scrignoli, *Invito all'ascolto di Mozart*, Mursia, Milano 1991; Joseph Solman, *Mozartiana. Due secoli di commenti, citazioni e aneddoti*, Longanesi, Milano 1991; Luciano Sterpellone, *Mozart tra medici e medicine*, Edizioni Paoline, Cinisello Balsamo (MI) 1991; Armando Torno e Pierangelo Sequeri, *Divertimenti per Dio. Mozart e i teologi*, Piemme, Casale Monferrato (AL) 1991; Hans Küng, *Mozart. Tracce della trascendenza*, Queriniana, Milano 1992; Amedeo Poggi ed Edgar Vallora, *Mozart. Signori, il catalogo è questo (Dal K 1 al K 626: l'analisi ragionata di tutte le composizioni)*, Einaudi, Torino 1992; Hermann Cohen, *L'idea drammatica di Mozart*, Marietti, Genova 1992; Stendhal, *Vita di Mozart*, Passigli, Firenze 1995; Georg Knepler, *W. Amadé Mozart. Nuovi percorsi*, Ricordi/LIM, Milano 1995; Maynard Solomon, *Mozart*, Mondadori, Milano 2006; Norbert Elias, *Mozart, sociologia di un genio*, by M.Schröter, Il Mulino, Bologna, 2005; Peter Gay, *Mozart: una biografia*, Fazi, Roma 2006; Sandro Cappelletto, *La notte delle dissonanze*, EDT, Torino 2006. Roman Vlad recorded a quick profile of Mozart in the «Mondadori Audiobooks»: *Per ascoltare Mozart*, Mondadori, Milano 1977. Moreover, it's worth to be mentioned the great work (in three books) by Hermann Abert, *Mozart*, Il Saggiatore, Milano 1984-86. Very interesting the epistolary: *Mozart, Autobiografia dalle lettere*, by Rosario F. Esposito, Edizioni Paoline, Catania 1960. A quick but intense profile of Mozart can be also found in Attilio Andrea Baratti, *Profili di musicisti*, La Zagara, Milano/Napoli 1959, pages 43-57.

In order to get acquainted with Mozart's instrumental masterpieces, I found the two books by Luigi Della Croce as fundamental: *Le 75 sinfonie di Mozart. Guida e analisi critica*, EDA, Torino 1977, and *I concerti di Mozart. Guida all'ascolto*, Mondadori, Milano 1983; and, for the piano production: Michèle Reverdy, *L'oeuvre pour piano de Mozart*, Paris 1978.

About the opera music, I suggest: Massimo Mila, *Il Flauto magico di Mozart*, Giappichelli, Torino 1977; Idem, *Lettura delle Nozze di Figaro*, Einaudi, Torino 1979; Idem, *Lettura del Don Giovanni*, Einaudi, Torino 1988; Stefan Kunze, *Il teatro di Mozart. Dalla «Finta semplice» al «Flauto magico»*, Marsilio, Venezia 1990.

Moreover, the contribution by François de Médicis, *Le convenzioni operistiche del XVIII secolo e le opere liriche di Mozart*, in Enciclopedia della musica, by Jacques Nattiez, Einaudi, Torino 2004, vol. IV, pages 658-681, is very interesting.

LUDWIG VAN BEETHOVEN
(1770-1827)

At the roots of human being.
A firm assertor of freedom and brotherhood

Portrait of Ludwig Van Beethoven while composing the "Missa Solemnis",
by Joseph Stieler, 1819. Archiv für Kunst und Geschichte.

From the «Field of Chards» to the Court of Prince Elector

Ludwig van Beethoven was born on December 16th, 1770 in Bonn. His family was of Flemish origin: in his surname denotes the particle "van", which is typical of the Flemish surnames (and which should not be confused with the "von" particle of the German surnames). In Flemish *beet-hoven* means "field of chards". And indeed it was a family of peasants, whose generations lived first in Leuven, then in Malines. From there the grandfather of the musician (also called Ludwig and also a musician by profession) had moved to Bonn, joining the palatine chapel of the prince elector of Cologne as bass and violinist.

His son Johann had followed the same path, working there as a tenor: he was, however, a less righteous person than his father, had a not good reputation and was devoted to drinking. He married a maid, a gentle woman, submissive, capable of immense endurance and, unfortunately, undermined by tuberculosis. The couple had seven children, four of whom died at an early age. The woman experienced marriage as a burden and a pain.

Ludwig found himself the greatest of the three surviving sons. He carried the name of his grandfather and showed great aptitude for music: so that his father, with the intent to make a new little Mozart, subjected him to inhumane methods of study to exhibit him as a child prodigy; and he also exhibited his son to the public pretending that he was two years younger than the real age.

Ludwig performed his first concerts at the age of eight. But the triumphs experienced by Mozart were not repeated for him. Until then he had very mediocre teachers, and the first real teacher was Neefe, a cultured and open musician, fond of Bach and Mozart, who was appointed organist of the Court of Cologne in 1782, when Ludwig was twelve years old. Neefe set a very serious study for the young Beethoven, based on Bach's well-tempered harpsichord, and supported him to get introduced into the court ambience. In 1784 the Grand Duke Maximilian-Franz, brother of the emperor, became prince-archbishop of Cologne. He was an enlightened reformer and a lover of music. He named the young Ludwig, then fourteen, second court organist: an extraordinary event for such a young boy.

In the meantime, Ludwig had also been introduced by his childhood friend Wegeler to the Breuning family: Elena Breuning was a cultured woman, widowed with four still young children; there was a need to give music lessons to those children, and Beethoven was in charge of it. He was immediately treated as a son: for him, a closed and difficult boy, who came from a family with many problems, it was a fundamental experience. Moreover, in Elena Breuning's living room (to which the boy was admitted despite his young age) there was talk of poetry and literature, art and philosophy; and the ideas of the most modern European culture flew.

The catalog of Beethoven works starts with the three *Trios* op. 1 (for piano, violin and cello) and the three *Piano Sonatas* op. 2. These are compositions that were published in 1795-96 but which were probably conceived in previous years: they are influenced by the eighteenth-century style, but in some passages they allow new horizons to be glimpsed because at times they reveal original ideas that detach themselves from the models of the period. It is interesting to hear some of them, bearing in mind that - as Giorgio Pestelli said - distinguishing the "three styles" in Beethoven's production helps us to look at Beethoven from above, drawing a picture of the evolving man, but this doesn't do justice to completeness of the first works.

AN EUROPE IN MOTION

When Beethoven was born, Europe is traversed by the ferments of the Enlightenment and in France the French Revolution approaches. Rousseau and Voltaire are still alive (both will die in 1778). Mozart is fourteen years old, Goethe is twenty-one and will soon publish *The Sorrows of Young Werther*. Schiller is eleven years old. Kant is forty-six, and in that year (1770) he got tenure of logic and metaphysics at the University of Königsberg: he published the precritical writings and the decade of silence is starting from which, in 1781, the *Critics of pure reason*, destined to produce a real Copernican revolution in philosophy. Schelling is five years old; Hegel was born in that year (he is therefore the same age as Beethoven). Lessing, the anticipator of the romantic turnaround, is at the height of his activity (he will die in 1781).

It is an Europe in motion. At all levels, subjectivity is emerging, that is, the value of the human person, of his reason, of his feeling.

The repercussions are on the institutions, from the civil to the religious ones, so often allied with each other in maintaining a *status quo* which benefits from narrow noble oligarchies and which cuts off immense masses of humble and dispossessed from social life: those masses on the whose sacrifice and on whose skin the powerful people have made official history, interwoven with wars, massacres, political games, and relations of power.

Beethoven catches these ferments: first in the Breuning living room, then through intense readings, later through enrollment at the University of Bonn (which was founded in 1786).

In the meantime he has won the esteem and sympathy of Count Waldstein, a young nobleman who is very influential at court and who, admirer of the young musician, gives him a piano and obtains for him by the prince the permission for a study trip to Vienna. The trip took place in 1787, and it seems that during the stop in Vienna Beethoven met Mozart, who would have said about him: "This boy will make the world talk about himself". In Vienna Beethoven succeeds as a concert artist, but the staying is interrupted by a sad news: the mother is very ill. Beethoven rushes to Bonn and arrives in time to witness his mother's death.

A very hard period follows. The father is stunned with alcohol and often gets drunk around, without being able to go home alone. At night Ludwig is forced to go around the city's taverns to look for the drunken father, load him on his shoulders and bring him home. The father is then deprived of parental authority, and Ludwig - nineteen years old – finds himself to be the head of the family, with the responsibility of two younger brothers. It is 1789.

«RECEIVE FROM HAYDN'S HANDS
THE HERITAGE OF MOZART»

Year 1789 is important not only for these serious responsibilities. It is also important because Beethoven enrolled in the faculty of Humanities and Philosophy at the University of Bonn. But it is important above all because it is the year in which the French Revolution breaks out.

The University of Bonn is open to all the avant-garde cultural currents. There are professors who are passionate supporters of the

French Revolution. Beethoven reads and studies a lot. It has the cult of Greekness: he loves Homer (both the *Iliad* and the *Odyssey*) and Plutarch (greedily reads the *Parallel Lives*). He loves the Enlightenmentists, especially Rousseau, Voltaire and the authors who most directly influenced the preparation of the French Revolution. He combines the works of Goethe, Schiller, Klopstock and other contemporary German poets. He became acquainted with English poets: from Shakespeare and Ossian to Milton. He studies Kant's thought and becomes an admirer of him.

Beethoven is therefore a musician fully integrated into the culture of his time. This is a fact, in some ways, new. Until then, musicians did not generally have a vast culture: they had broad and deep musical knowledge, but their culture stopped there, on a specialized level. Of course, Händel also enrolled at the University, and Mozart had in his library books by Goethe, Lessing, and Torquato Tasso. But Beethoven is the first musician to feel the need to catch up with the poet, the playwright, the philosopher and to be part of the culture of his time.

This basic orientation will never be abandoned, even with the interruption of university studies. Those studies do not last long because in 1792 the great and famous Haydn passes from Bonn, coming from England, and celebrations are organized for him. During these celebrations, Haydn hears Beethoven playing; he understands his skills and offers to give him lessons in Vienna. Beethoven leaves for the Austrian capital, supported by good wishes of friends.

Among his best friends there is Waldstein, who wishes Beethoven to "receive from the hands of Haydn the heritage of Mozart" (Mozart died a few months ago). It is a truly prophetic wish: even if Beethoven will receive from Haydn very few lessons, due to the rising of an immediately apparent and marked incompatibility, on the human level as on the artistic level, between the two musicians, and Beethoven will soon abandon Haydn, revealed a teacher not careful and scarcely solicitous towards him. In memory of this relationship we remember, curiously, the epithet of "Gran Mogol" (emperor of the Mongols), that Haydn used to describe the young musician: an epithet rather well chosen (although far from being kind), taking into account the appearance Beethoven's physique (olive complexion, not tall, rather stocky, with a face pocked with traces of smallpox) and his rather reactive, unfriendly and rebellious character.

In Vienna, Beethoven gathers again a huge success as a pianist. But even his compositions are beginning to be appreciated. He gets the esteem and admiration of some nobles, among whom are already distinguished the names of those who will be for him very attached protectors: Prince Lobkowitz, Prince Lichnowsky, Count von Fries, Prince Schwarzenberg, Countess Thun, the baron van Swieten. But above all, Beethoven becomes music teacher of Archduke Rodolfo, brother of the emperor, who will remain bound to him by affectionate veneration.

Among the compositions that Beethoven performs in Vienna there are the *Concerts for piano and orchestra* n. 1 op. 15 and n. 2 op. 19.

I propose to listen to the first movement of the *Concert op. 15* and the last movement of the *Concert op. 19*. We are faced with brilliant music of entertainment, according to the style of the era. However, we feel, in some passages and in some echoes, something new, strong, I dare to say of leonine: a certain way of making music that shakes inside, and above all a tumult of ideas and a dramatic comparison between piano and orchestra that they announce substantial news. Beethoven is twenty-five years old and is already detached from the Haydnian and Mozart models. It belongs to this period also the *Settimino op. 20* (so called because it is a composition for seven instruments: clarinet, horn, bassoon, violin, viola, cello and double bass), of which I recommend listening to the delicious *Minuetto*.

A «STRONG» MUSIC

Massimo Mila identifies a characteristic of Beethoven's music in strength. Strength understood not as violence, but as robustness, power, self-control, incisiveness, ability to move and drag. Even in the consistency of Mozart's heritage, there is in Beethoven - as we have mentioned - something genuinely new.

Mila makes some instructive examples, comparing the first movement of the *Sonata for piano op. 2 n. 1* by Beethoven and the last movement of Mozart's *Symphony K 550*; the second movement of Beethoven's *First Symphony* with the second movement of Mozart's same *Symphony K 550*.

And he highlights how some common thematic cells find new and absolutely unpredictable developments in Beethoven compared to those of Mozart. It is a very interesting comparison, because it shows how the same start can take very different paths depending on the temperament and inspiration of the composer. We could immediately verify what Mila says, listening in parallel to the pieces indicated. One understands, then, why some commentators have recognized in the Beethoven's *First Symphony* a sort of leave from the eighteenth century, that is, the first symptoms of the imminent decline of classicism; and why Paolo Gallarati has perceived in it a sound that he calls "perspective" and that makes the orchestra an unpublished character, endowed with a vitality and a force unknown before.

We could then listen to the first part of the Beethoven's *Second Symphony*. After a slow introduction of ascending and descending movements, a theme full of rhythmic strength begins: it proceeds snappy, and drags the listener in a pleasant and exciting run, developing and expanding in an increasingly engaging way, up to the festive and brilliant conclusion.

But that strength will explode especially in the *Eroica*, the *Third Symphony*, which constitutes an absolute *quid novi* in the field of symphonic music. Music ceases to have a hedonistic and famulative function (that is, a means of accompaniment to parties, entertainments, ceremonies of various kinds): it becomes a decisive spiritual message destined to reach the listener and to involve him directly. According to Eduardo Rescigno, the first performance of the Eroica has a historical significance, because it definitely realizes some anticipations that were just sketched in the *London Symphonies* of Haydn or in the last three Mozart symphonies: music ceases to have the utilitarian function of accompaniment for events of court or for religious ceremonies and becomes a free confession of a free artist, a message of intellectual, moral and educational content.

The particular history of the *Eroica* helps us to understand the meaning of this transformation. Beethoven had placed great hopes in Napoleon, whom he considered to be the heir to the French Revolution, as the one who would bring the ideals of freedom, equality, and fraternity to Europe. "Napoleon consul" was seen by him as one of the great Roman consuls. And Beethoven had Napoleon in mind when he had composed the *Third Symphony*, naming it precisely Bonaparte.

His disappointment was terrible when, on May 20th 1804, Napoleon proclaimed himself emperor, putting himself on the same level as the other powerful men of Europe and assuming the role of dictator. When the pupil Ries brought him the news of that proclamation to emperor, Beethoven was furious and shouted: «He too is nothing but an ordinary man! Now he will trample all human rights too, he will stand taller than anyone else, he will become a tyrant!» Then he took the sheet with the title of the symphony (Bonaparte) and cut it to pieces. Subsequently he titled that symphony *Sinfonia Eroica* composed for the memory of a great man (the "memory" of a person that no longer exists). For Beethoven, Napoleon had denied himself; he was therefore dead, he had disappeared from the horizon of hopes. From this standpoint, the *Funeral march* that constitutes the second movement of this symphony takes on a particular meaning: even if that page was written before the change of title, that change gives it a new and intense meaning, fully in line with the real feelings of Beethoven; and indeed the first London edition of the symphony (1809) bears the words: "Heroic Symphony composed to celebrate the death of a Hero".

Let's listen to the first and second movement of the *Eroica*. The first movement immediately reveals the characteristics I have stressed; the second is the famous *Funeral March* of which I said.

With the *Eroica* music enters life, becomes a political manifesto, becomes a spiritual message. And the message here is clearly perceptible: it is a fierce protest against the dictatorship, it is a clear line up for the freedom of the peoples, it is an affirmation of human rights. The "strong" language of this symphony is suitable for this type of message. It introduces a real revolution. In this symphony we also find dissonances that sound unacceptable for a classicist, but which have a very clear expressive function. Even the length of the symphony breaks the Haydnian scheme. And it is a length that is not prolixity; it is the result of the need to say many things and therefore the need to have a "vehicle" available to suit the urgency of the message. That vehicle is specially designed by Beethoven, of which Harold Schonberg rightly said that he was "a force of nature", a man who was sure of his genius and who, once an idea was made, walked in that direction with a musical infallible instinct.

A «POLITICAL» MUSIC

This "political" dimension of Beethoven's music ("political", not in the party sense, but in the sense of strong civil commitment) will remain a constant note of his artistic production. It is linked to the fact that Beethoven is the first musician who has not been a court official: since the beginning of his career he has been a free artist (Roland Barthes calls him "the first free man of music") and composed not on the order of clients, but obeying exclusively his spiritual urgencies. His patrons will be his friends, never masters. And this will give him much autonomy in moving on the "political" level and in launching, with his music, messages congenial to his *Weltanschauung*.

The idea of freedom remains, in Beethoven, a common thread that has deep roots and many ramifications in his works.

He was a tenacious and severe critic of absolutism; he expressed harsh judgments on the emperor and the imperial Hapsburg court (so much so that Schindler will arbitrary destroy - as a political precaution - as many as two hundred and forty "conversation notebooks", which I will discuss later). He had a deep admiration for England, as a country of secular affirmation of freedom, and had for all his life the desire, unfulfilled, to visit that country.

In 1813, when the English general Wellington (the future winner of Waterloo) defeated the French troops in Spain in the battle of Vitoria, Beethoven composed a commemorative piece entitled *The Victory of Wellington or the battle of Vitoria* (abbreviated: *The Battle of Wellington* or *The victory of Wellington*): it is a piece of circumstance, enormously inferior to the *Eroica*, but poses itself politically on the same line. It is a minor Beethoven, which indulges in spectacular aspects and cheap musical tricks (such as the use of cannon noise in the course of the composition): but it must also be known, also to demystify Beethoven and prove his music also has trends of weakness and surrenders to fashion. Similarly we find them in the *Glorious Moment*, a composition commissioned to him on the occasion of the Congress of Vienna (it is perhaps the only time that Beethoven has accepted a "commission" from the powerful people): here too, a composition of circumstance and scarce musical value, in which, perhaps, a note of opportunism is also visible.

I propose to listen to *The victory of Wellington* op. 91, which describes the preparation of the two armies, the development of the clash, the victory of the English, with the flourishing of the English national anthem and the succumbing of the Marseillaise: a piece full of color, with the stereo effect of the two opposing fanfares, with the use of bass drums and tree-frog instruments to imitate the blows

145

of the cannons and the crackling of the guns. I also propose to listen to a passage from the *Glorious Moment*, recalling that Beethoven was very much celebrated during the Congress of Vienna.

But these limitations should not make us forget that Beethoven's idea of freedom was truly a fundamental idea, for his life and his work, and inspired him to make great compositions. I want to mention the *Egmont*, an *overture* that Beethoven wrote for the music of the scene of the homonymous Goethe tragedy, centered on the figure of Egmont, the hero who fought in the sixteenth century against the Spanish for the freedom of the Flemish people (and it is understandable the passion that Beethoven put there, being of Flemish origin).

Let's listen to this *overture*, which is a mighty fresco where the themes of spiritual strength and struggle intertwine with the themes of love for women and love for one's nationals.

The dialectic freedom-tyranny finds its highest expression in the only work that Beethoven wrote for the theater and which he entitled: *Fidelio or Conjugal love.*

The protagonist is a woman, Leonora, whose husband Florestano has been imprisoned by the tyrant Pizarro; the woman dresses up as a man and takes the name of Fidelio in order to enter the prison and comfort her husband; the disguise has paradoxical effects, because the daughter of the jailer falls in love with the "boy" Leonora, and this creates complications; but Leonora manages to bring comfort to her husband and to defend him from Pizarro's attempt to kill him; the story then comes to a positive conclusion, because the tyrant will fall and the prisoners will be freed.

The work is an exaltation of freedom and, at the same time, of conjugal love. Very beautiful passages are: n. 10 (*Choir of the prisoners*); n. 11 (*Theme of Florestano*, intense and throbbing); n. 14 (Quartet between Florestano, Leonora, Pizarro and Rocco, called *Gun Quartet*); and the last piece, sung by the soloists and the choir (*O God, whose power*).

For this work Beethoven wrote four different overtures: dissatisfied with one, he tried another. There are, therefore, three overtures with the title *Leonora* (name that originally the composer wanted to give to the work) and a fourth with the title

Fidelio (name that is inspired by the fidelity of the conjugal and which then remained the definitive title).

«GOETHE LIKES TOO MUCH THE COURTLY ATMOSPHERE...»

This Beethoven's pride, this awareness of the value of his ideas and his art, the disdain for every kind of tyranny, the rejection of all forms of courtliness are expressed in an emblematic way in the meeting occurred in Töplitz, in 1812, between Beethoven, the emperor and Goethe.

From the stories we received, it appears that Beethoven had the opportunity to meet the emperor of Habsburg while he was walking. They all took wing at the king's passage and bowed deeply: first of all, Goethe. Beethoven, on the other hand, went on proudly on his way without even sketching a bow, and it was the emperor who greeted him first.

Dai racconti pervenutici, risulta che Beethoven ebbe occasione di incontrare colà l'imperatore di Asburgo mentre stava passeggiando. Tutti fecero ala al passaggio del sovrano e si inchinarono profondamente: primo fra tutti, Goethe. Beethoven, invece, proseguì con fierezza per la sua strada senza neanche abbozzare un inchino, e fu l'imperatore a salutarlo per primo.

Beethoven will comment, in one of his letters:

«Goethe, likes too much courtly atmosphere; he likes more than what is appropriate for a poet. There is not much more to say about the ridiculousness of virtuosos, that is, of musicians who play only to amaze with their ability, when poets who should be considered as the first masters of the nation forget everything for these frills».

In fact Goethe, who had met Napoleon in Erfurt four years earlier and had called him "my emperor", had a spirit and style as a courtier (and besides he was a man of the court, because for many years he held the role of first minister at the court of the Grand Duke of Weimar). Perhaps Beethoven had more than one meeting with Goethe. But the two did not understand each other. They were too different and Beethoven's music was too new for a man like Goethe, who had a musical sensibility linked to rather ancient and cramped schemes. He, the "Olympic poet", hated "disorder" and revolution, despite having been one of the protagonists of the Sturm und Drang in his youth.

He declared himself «stunned» by Beethoven's genius and said he had never seen an artist «more powerfully concentrated (*zusammengefasster*), more energetic, more profound»; but he defined it as a personality «unfortunately totally unbridled (*ungehändigte*)».

And when, later on, the young Mendelssohn will make him hear the first movement of Beethoven's *Fifth Symphony* on the piano, Goethe will say: «It's a great thing, really crazy... You're afraid your house is collapsing on you... Imagine if the whole orchestra were to perform it!» And Zelter, Goethe's musical advisor, will define Beethoven as «a Hercules who uses the cudgel to drive away flies».

A SONATA THAT BECOMES A DRAMA

The piano sonata *Aurora* op. 53 belongs to the same period of the *Eroica Symphony*. This sonata is also called *Waldsteinsonate* because it is dedicated to Waldstein, friend and patron of Beethoven.

We find here again a big transformation with respect to Haydn or Mozart. Some dramatic flashes that had passed through the last Mozart sonatas become the background color of Beethoven's composition. The two themes on which the traditional sonata form is set become two protagonists who confront and clash. The sonata becomes drama, a clash between two principles: the opposing and repelling principle (*widerstrabende Prinzip*) and the begging principle (*bittende Prinzip*). According to the Beethoven scholars, there is here a dualism of principles which is proper to Kant's precritical philosophy (Beethoven knew Kant's precritical writings). The title *Aurora* was given to the sonata for some particularity of atmosphere, which Alfredo Casella effectively summarizes in this way: «From a deaf sonority rises this flash of dazzling light».

And that's true. The first movement starts from an indistinct harmonic background that - Eduardo Rescigno says - is just mentioned and could belong to a piano exercise for the looseness of the wrist; then that harmonic background becomes more and more distinct, the various elements are organized, the tone changes; this change is like an opening of brightness and leads to a second theme that has the flavor of a choir and has an open melodiousness. The second movement, dark and mysterious, set on very few notes that evoke the quail song, is very short and soon passes into the third movement, which is a very fast *Rondò*, with a popular flavor: it sings richly and draws to the top of joy, ending with cascades of trills and mighty final chords.

Following the araising of the themes, their intertwining and developing, enjoying the change in tone, participating in the progressive struggle through which the composer comes to the conclusion, means being involved in a thrilling and exciting adventure. This adventure becomes a constant feature of all Beethoven's sonatas: in particular the *Appassionata* and the sonata *Les adieux*; but it was already clearly perceptible in the *Patetica*.

Let's listen to the sonata *Aurora* trying to grasp the elements that we have briefly indicated.

WALLED INTO SILENCE

Between 1796 and 1800 a strange phenomenon developed in Beethoven: first it manifests as a whistle in the ears, then like a waterfall noise. It is an extremely uncomfortable condition for a musician, as it pollutes his perception of sounds. Unfortunately, the phenomenon does not cease, rather it worsens. Beethoven begins to no longer hear the voices of others. In the spring of 1801 he plays the «pianissimo» so whispered that no sound comes out of the instrument: he plays without sounding; and he does not notice this. In the countryside he sees a shepherd playing the flute and asks those around him: "Why does not he play?". Hearing is now strongly compromised. Beethoven quickly falls to deafness.

It's a terrible misfortune, especially for a musician. Beethoven tries to conceal from the others the disease that torments him: he feels diminished, dejected; he is ashamed of his handicap. But above all he is tormented by the awareness that he is losing touch with the world of sounds, his world: a vital world for a musician.

He will use every possible cure to try to stop deafness. But the primitive medicine of that time did not have anything to recommend but compresses, cold water baths, or baths in lukewarm water of the Danube (!!!). And then, the use of bigger and bigger cornets, in an effort to cling as far as possible to the world of sounds. And when the cornets are no longer effective, Beethoven tries to remedy using an iron rod held between his teeth and resting on the piano case in a desperate attempt to "suck" from the instrument, mechanically, those vibrations that could no longer be perceived by ears.

It is an immense drama. Beethoven will no longer be able to conduct an orchestra, because, not hearing the instruments, his conduction will turn into chaos. When the first performance of the *Ninth Symphony* will take place - directed by another musician, present the author in the first row - the theater will reverberate with applause, but Beethoven will not hear anything, and they will have to take him by the shoulders and turn him towards the audience in delirium in order to make him realize that his symphony had been successful.

He remains walled in his silence. He still manages to compose, because a great musician does not need to physically hear the music he composes: he "feels" it ideally in his mind, conceives it and writes it as conceived; but he will never have the joy of listening to its execution. An atrocious handicap.

And even in his relationship with others will be blocked by this tremendous handicap. He no longer has the possibility of a direct talk: those who speak to him must write in a notebook what they say or ask, and let him read it; and only after reading, Beethoven will be able to respond aloud.

Thus, the "conversation notebooks" are born: documents of extreme historical interest, which offer us a glimpse of Beethoven's inner world.

It is only a partial glimmer, because the notebooks record only the questions of the interlocutors and not Beethoven's answers; they therefore offer us a sort of "negative cast" of the great musician's speeches. But they are still precious documents, which inform us about the subjects that Beethoven used to talk about. It is regrettable that many of them were not preserved because Schindler, a pupil of Beethoven and acting as his secretary, believed them to be scarcely interesting or too compromising and - lacking respect for the Master's memory - then arbitrarily decided to destroy them.

«Durch Leiden, Freude»
(«Through pain, happiness»)

In this climate, Beethoven's "philosophy" grows up: not to be overthrown by adversity, to affirm the strength of the human spirit, to conquer joy through pain *(Durch Leiden, Freude*: "Through pain, joy!"). From Beethoven's standpoint, joy is not the expression of hedonism nor the fruit of fortune: it is the purpose of moral action and a reward for commitment; it is what brings man to God and connects him to other men as brothers. Pain is a step of this itinerary.

Of this intense dialectic, of this centrality of man, of this struggle to affirm the strength of reason over the irrationality of evil and of "necessity", the *Fifth Symphony* is a very high document. It expresses an internalization of the struggle expressed in the *Third Symphony*; and expresses, at the same time, an essentialization of the musical discourse, which becomes more concise, more dense, more tense. It has been called *Sinfonia del Destino* (Symphony of the Destiny) because all the first movement is rhythmized on a four-note thematic cell (tà-tatà-tà): four notes which are four robust strokes, in order to which Beethoven, questioned about their meaning, said: «Thus Destiny knocks at the door».

On those four notes a vigorous discourse develops, followed by a second theme, sweet and melodious, which soon becomes overwhelmed by the first theme.

The second movement is an *Andante con moto* that unveils a sweet and beautiful theme, of an elegiac nature, sung by violas and cellos and then taken over by the orchestra. The third movement has the rhythm of a *Scherzo*, mysterious and strange; the thematic cell of the first movement reappears. The transition from the third to the fourth movement takes place without interruption: the passage occurs through a shaky and seething sound magma, which slowly organizes and coagulates, generating, almost miraculously, a clear, strong, heroic theme, one could say titanic. It is a theme that advances and urges, triumphant and solemn. It is a theme that warms the heart and instills joy and optimism: the joy of those who have conquered the adverse destiny, affirming the power of rationality and courage. A very human poem, therefore, this *Fifth Symphony*: a poem in which each one finds something of his own human story.

Here again the influence of Kant emerges, both for the space that this philosopher has given to subjectivity, shifting the focus of the "problem of knowledge" from the world of objects to the world of the subject, both for the conception of the moral law, seen as law autonomous (that is, as a law that springs from the very structure of man) and as the realm of freedom, opposed to nature (which is instead the world dominated by necessity). «Being free means to want what is owed». In Beethoven's "philosophy" this truth is expressed as follows: in front necessity (Destiny) the force of reason must be established, affirming the freedom of man. On the score of his last quartet, Beethoven wrote: «*Es muss sein*» («It must be»). It seems to me a variant of the categorical Kantian imperative.

Not for nothing, in the notes of Beethoven is the sentence: «The starry sky above me, the moral law within me». It is a fragment of the phrase that Kant wrote in the last pages of the *Critique of Practical Reason*: "Two things fill me with wonder: above me the starry sky, within me the moral law".

This "kantism" is expressed not only in the Beethoven symphonies, but also in some piano sonatas and many other compositions.

We can listen to the first and the second movement of the *Sonata Patetica* op. 13. It has been called "patetica" by Beethoven himself; in Kant's language this word does not mean "sentimental", but (I quote here some words of the poet Schiller, another Kant's lover) "tragic force of representation through which the freedom of spirit, in a heroic ethical imperative, can reach the overcoming of pain". The *Patetica* is very famous and is perhaps one of the Beethoven sonatas in which the dynamics of Beethoven's thought are more clearly and emblematically presented.

We could also mention here the *Kreutzer Sonata* (piano and violin sonata, which takes its name from the fact that Beethoven dedicated it to the violinist Rodolfo Kreutzer). The opening *Presto* is of great beauty: Giovanni Carli Ballola says that it is dominated by the overwhelming and impetuous inspiration of the years of Beethoven heroic voluntarism, and adds: «Never before has the dialectic concertante for piano and violin been so thick, exasperated and stretched to the spasm, neither the writing of the two instruments had reached such a degree of virtuosic splendor and of powerful expressive aspect». Tolstoy borrowed from this *Sonata* the title for a famous novel, whose protagonist suspects that his wife (expert pianist) betrays him with a violinist with whom she gives concerts playing the *Kreutzer Sonata*; the man will believe to find confirmation of the betrayal when, unexpectedly going back home from a trip, he finds the violinist at dinner with the woman. In a raptus of jealousy and revenge he kills his wife. In the novel Tolstoy attacks marriage, asserting that it is a hypocritical institution and source of suffering and arguing that abstention from sexual relations is the only way to build a more human world and to implement true Christianity. This, of course, aroused much controversy and Tolstoy felt the need to defend himself, adding to the book an "afterword", containing long dissertations about the practicality of sexual continence and about the vices of society that with every type of intervention (including art) approves and leads to sexual intercourse. Singular thing: in this afterword the writer makes no mention of the *Kreutzer Sonata*. This is explicitly mentioned only in a page of the twenty-third chapter of the novel: describing a concert in which the protagonist assists and in which his wife and violinist perform the *Sonata*, Tolstoj comments on a piece of the same *Sonata* (which is the *Presto* of the first movement) in this way: «Is it possible to play it in a living room among ladies with low-cut dresses? Play, then applaud, then eat ice cream and talk about the latest gossip? Similar pieces can only be performed under certain important and significant circumstances... ». In the reference to "ladies with low-cut dresses", many readers (and several commentators) immediately saw an allusion to the eroticism and immorality to which that music would excite. But, in my opinion, the context of the page sounds very different: it expresses a very high esteem for the music of Beethoven and stresses that it is not to be performed in frivolous environments (characterized by social life, low-cut women, gossip, bingeing, etc.) because it is music that "speaks to the soul" (textual words by Tolstoy), opens new dimensions, transforms human relationships: to the point that the protagonist of the novel (a man who has a demeaning conception of marriage and who until then lived in a materialistic way) for the first time understands that his wife is a human being equal to him and feels towards her «of new feelings, never tried before».

The music allowed him, therefore, to do a great discovery and changed his relationship with his wife: he humanized and ennobled him, raising him to a previously unimaginable level. What emerges from the Tolstoyan page therefore appears to be in line with Beethoven's ethics. What then those positive effects of the *Sonata* did not have long duration in the protagonist of the story, it seems to me that it concerns another matter.

A Short Season of Serenity:
The Fourth, the Sixth and the Eighth Symphony

Beethoven's life and work are not always and only "fighting against adverse destiny". There are periods in which a clear serenity dominates.

Beethoven's affective life was certainly not happy, but had peaceful moments. He fell in love with many women: with Giulietta Guicciardi, with Teresa Brunswick and with her sister Giuseppina, with Teresa Malfatti, with Bettina Brentano, with Amalia Sebald. He was not handsome, but he attracted by the force of his figure and his personality. In 1806, according to a biographical tradition, he secretly got engaged with Teresa Brunswick, with the consent of her brother, but without the consent of the parents; according to a more recent thesis, based on the discovery of new letters, he would not have been engaged to Teresa, but would have loved her sister Giuseppina (and some biographer suggested that Giuseppina had a daughter from him). The fact is that 1806 was a time of great joy: the *Fourth Symphony* (so happy and light), the *Sixth Symphony* (called *Pastorale*) and the *Sonata Appassionata* was born.

I propose to listen to the *Fourth Symphony*. Carli Ballola has defined it as "the triumph of the wood instruments, which with their soft and luminous doughs and their stylistic sorties dominate almost everywhere in the first movement". Then we listen to the first movement, sweet and flowing like "living water among the pebbles of a stream", and the last movement, "a masterpiece of animated orchestral virtuosity, from the beginning to the end, from an intimate joy of the spirit".

Even in other periods we have serene pages: moments of relaxation and serenity that seem without struggle. For example: in 1802, the *Romanza for violin and orchestra* op. 50 and, in 1812, the *Eighth Symphony*.

Let's listen to the delicious *Romanza op. 50* and the exquisite second movement of the *Eighth Symphony*: it is a very funny, joking *Allegretto*, in which Beethoven has retraced a joking piece that he had composed for Mälzel, the perfecter of the metronome; it is a passage in which the metronome ticking is parodied. The third movement is a *Minuetto*, also set in a parodic tone: it is worth listening to it.

Also the *Sixth Symphony* belongs to a similar period, even if a few years later. It is a poem of nature. Its five movements depict a "story" of the relationship between man and nature. Beethoven was a lover of nature: his letters and biographical information gathered from his friends describe him as a lover of the countryside, thirsty for greenery, rapt in the contemplation of the trees, the sky, the flowing water. Although the various movements of the symphony were labelled with a caption by Beethoven himself, he wrote at the top of the score this phrase: «More expression of sensations than painting». With this he intended to exclude that the symphony had a descriptive character and intended to affirm the Kantian principle according to which art is not an imitation of nature but a spontaneous and subjective creation of man.

The "story" begins with the arrival in the country and with the "playful feelings" that it awakens. The first movement is set on a fresh and sparkling theme, very relaxing. It evokes the sense of peace experienced by those leaving the city (especially today, with the chaotic and polluted cities in which we live) and entering another world, where the dimensions are different, where everything is more human, where the rhythms are at measure of man, where plunging into the green is oxygenating and life-giving.

The second movement is titled "Scene on the bank of a stream" and evokes the sense of rapture of those who are filled by the voices of nature, listen to them, enjoy them, and draw them as food for the life of the spirit. And those voices are the voices of the water and the leaves, of the nightingale and of the quail and of the cuckoo: all together they form a concert that relaxes and recreates. In particular, the song of the quail is evocative, whose scheme (tàa-ta-tà) had already been used by Beethoven in the second half of the *Sonata Aurora*. Luigi Magnani highlighted its close kinship with the theme of Beethoven's lied *The song of the quail*, a theme translated in the words "*Lobe Gott, liebe Gott, danke Gott*" ("Praise God, love God, thank God").

The third movement (Happy peasant gathering) is animated by the presence of man, who is placed in that context as a co-protagonist: a simple and frank type of man, whose presence does not clash and violate nature, but rather fits with perfect harmony and coherence between the natural elements referred to in the first and second movement, elements in front of which man had been simply a spectator so far. It is a group of farmers and peasants who dance to the sound of pastoral instruments. The dance is cheerful, festive, of a healthy and rustic joy: it is certainly not refined; it is typically popular and with passages that in Piedmontese would be called "a supatùn". The theme is played by the oboe with bassotuba accompaniment.

The happy dance has a moment of suspension when you hear the rumbling of a distant thunder; but then he resumes carefree, with the mood of someone who drives away a troubling concern. Other rumblings are heard and followed by other suspensions; then the first drops fall, and then the dance quickly falls into a labored rhythm and into a general escape. The storm is unleashed and dominates with the spectacle of thunder, lightning, showers (it is the fourth movement). But it never makes a noise: it is all music, even in the climax of more violent acme. Particularly effective is the whistling of the wind (evoked by the most acute registers of the orchestra: flutes and octaves) and the zig-zagging of the lightning, evoked by the drawings, descending in zig-zag, of the arches. Certain sounds, then, have the livid color of lightning. The storm is short, although violent. It moves away quickly, with the last thunderclaps, with the last showers of water, now dim. And the serene reappears on the dripping nature of water. In the clean and rarefied air, smelling of humidity, the sun reappears, and from the immense chorus of the renewed nature, of the animals out of their dens, of the men returned from their shelters in the open air, rises to the Creator a hymn of thanksgiving.

The orchestra expresses this chorality with accents in which it sometimes looks like an immense organ, celebrating gratitude to God and the joy of rediscovered peace. It is the fifth movement, which closes the symphony. It can also be read as a celebration of peace between man and nature, between man and other men, achieved through the definitive overcoming of the hurricane of war: an apologue of the arduous journey of humanity towards goals of rationality and universal brotherhood. These are goals that are unfortunately still very far today, both in terms of wars of all kinds, and about the ecological problems and the ruthless exploitation of many populations in developing countries.

Between the third, fourth and fifth movements of this symphony there is no break in continuity.

THE MYSTERY OF THE «IMMORTAL BELOVED»

But these periods of serenity are, in truth, very rare. In the life and work of Beethoven, the pain and struggle of which we have spoken are dominant.

Deafness makes him suspicious, scorbutic, nervous, misanthropic. He dreams of forming a family, but his life will take place in solitude, in the mess of a single man house, in the hands of housekeepers that he will change continuously (no housekeeper could bear him for long), moving dozens of times because always dissatisfied with the arrangement and always in conflict with neighbors because of his grumpy character.

In the life of Beethoven, a significant relationship with the woman was missing. He always had the deep nostalgia of a woman beside him, the nostalgia for marriage, the nostalgia for fatherhood. As we have already mentioned, there were many affections that went through his life, with varying intensity. But none of them could be realized in a project of a life together. Perhaps the decisive influence on his sentimental affairs was the torment of deafness and the concern to tie a woman to that terrible misfortune, which isolated and excluded him from a normal life of relationship.

But there are those who think that, in the unconscious, he was profoundly misogynist and that, precisely because of that, he fell in love only with women who under no circumstances would have married him. It is not unlikely, then, that the negative experience of childhood, lived in the reality of a failed marriage and in the veneration of a mother who was lost very soon, influenced his love life.

Beethoven's sentimental events have immediate reflections on his music. The intense fusion between life and work is an essential characteristic of Beethovenian art, which anticipates romantic conception.

For example, the love for Giulietta Guicciardi is reflected in the *Moonlight Sonata*, which is dedicated to her.

We can immediately listen to the *Moonlight Sonata*. It derives its singular name from the fact that the first movement is based on an insistent drawing of tercets played by the left hand and on which a heartfelt melody is grafted: that drawing of tercets has suggested to the poet Rellstab the image of the moon's glitter on Lake of the Four Cantons, and from this derives the title with which the piano masterpiece is indicated. The "loving" context must not, however, condition or limit the understanding of the sonata: which is, above all, an extraordinary synthesis of Beethovenian philosophy. Starting from an abyss of pain, restrained and profound (the great pianist Cortot said: «A pain that, in its intensity, falls back on itself and is destroyed»), the sonata gradually rises, arriving, through a stringent and robust dialectic, to the heroic tones of the highest spiritual temperament that are proper to the third movement.

The same must be said for the *Sonata Appassionata* op. 57, whose title, given by a publisher, is apt, because it is a sonata shaken by waves of intense passion.

In Beethoven's biography there is a mysterious and exceptional document: the *Letter to the Immortal Beloved*. It is an intensely passionate letter, which ends with the famous phrase: "Eternally yours, eternally mine, eternally ours". The biographers have indulged in the search for the woman to whom the Immortal Beloved would correspond. Various hypotheses have been made, but the elements that support each hypothesis can be countered and neutralized by opposite proofs. There is no need to deal with this controversy.

The *Letter to the Immortal Beloved* can be considered the twin of another fundamental document of Beethoven's biography: the so-called *Testament of Heiligenstadt*. It is called "testament" because it is a letter addressed by Beethoven to his brothers with the imperious phrase: "To be read after my death". The letter was written in Heiligenstadt, a village outside Vienna (today a suburb of the capital), in which Beethoven had gone to stay on the advice of the doctor, hoping to cure deafness. It was found in a drawer, after his death. It is an immense cry of sorrow, and at the same time a cry of hope because the letter ends with the expression: "O Providence, make that at least one day of pure joy shines for me".

The two documents are ten years far: the testament is dated 1802, the letter to the Immortal Beloved is dated 1812. They constitute two important stages to penetrate the inner world of Beethoven.

In November 1815 one of Beethoven's brothers, Kaspar Karl, died, left a nine-year-old son, Karl, explicitly assigning the child's protection to his mother and uncle Ludwig. Beethoven never valued his brother's wife and now does not want to share Karl's protection with her. But the woman claims to exercise her rights as a mother of the boy. A judicial dispute follows, which will last a long time and that Beethoven will definitely win in 1820.

A paternal feeling is triggered in him; his secret dream of a family and of fatherhood finds, in that affair, a sudden possibility of partial fulfillment. This feeling is combined with the aversion to the boy's mother and leads him to engage deeply in the long controversy, which will take away a lot of money and cause him many anxieties. The relationship with his sister-in-law is interpreted by someone in the key of aversion-attraction: a sort of hate-love that would find its roots in the unsolved knot of Beethoven's relationship with the female reality.

Anyway, the boy will grow up far from his uncle's wishes: he will grow up rather rebellious, liar, wasteful, lazy in his studies; he will flee from the colleges in which he will be placed; he will attend companies that are not recommended; he will end up attempting suicide. He will therefore be a source of infinite sorrow for the uncle, who will be disappointed by the great emotional investment made on him, but will not cease to love him, to forgive him, to help him.

They wrote a lot about Beethoven's nephew and the pain he gave his uncle. However, it is realistic to consider that Karl was certainly not in the best conditions to grow in a calm and balanced way. Orphaned by his father when he was still young, he found himself in the difficult situation of all the children disputed between relatives and devastated by that conflict.

Karl was severely involved in the intense conflict between his mother and uncle, creating an inner laceration that certainly did not help his psycho-affective balance. It is conceivable that he was inclined towards his mother and that he was hostile to that rigorous and obstinate uncle who took him from his mother and put him in boarding school. The developments of the story led him to a refusal to his uncle: especially since Beethoven, as we said, was a very difficult character, and had to be a very heavy, overprotective, asphyxiating uncle-tutor. He was a man endowed with strong moral principles, but unable to immerse himself in the psychology of a boy and to set up an educational action responding to the real needs of an adolescent. This deficiency could not be adequately compensated by the affection - real and sincere - that he had for the boy. This explains, in my opinion, its failure on the educational level.

THE «THEME»: A PERSON WHO GROWS AND BECOMES ADULT

This failure against his nephew was therefore one of the adversities through which Beethoven had to pass to win his fight with destiny and to conquer, despite everything, joy. That struggle is - as we have said - the spring, the soul of much of his work: we have seen its reflections in the piano and symphonic compositions. We would like to remind you that the same dialectic animates the concerts for piano and orchestra, the trios, the quartets.

Piano concerts are, like the symphonies, an extraordinarily significant constellation in Beethovenian production. There are five in all (apart from fragments of a sixth); of these, the third, fourth and fifth, which belong to the musician's maturity, are especially important. It has been said that they are so famous that they can "walk in group" without losing their identity. It has also been said that they stop at the threshold of the last Beethoven style and do not cover the years after 1810 because, due to deafness, Beethoven lacked the primary impulse to the composition of this type of music, based on the solo performance of pianist-author.

The *Fifth concert op. 53* is the brilliant *Concert of the emperor*, whose breadth and symphonic development are remarkable. Its name was not given by Beethoven and was coined after the composer's death: its origin is not clear; some say that at the first Viennese execution a French officer called him "the emperor of concerts"; others attributes to a publisher the choice of the name. Anyway, this qualification documents the kind of success that the concert received.

Personally, I prefer the *Fourth concert op. 58*, more tender, richer in nuances, I would say more perfect; and especially the second movement, in which there is an intense and touching dialogue between the piano and the orchestra. The piano seems to embody the imploring principle and to ask restless and hesitant questions, to which the orchestra, with its robust and incisive voice, provides drastic, imperious, unequivocal answers. In my opinion it is a very special and extremely suggestive version of Beethoven's dualism.

This dualism is expressed here in an emblematic way because of the pressing intensity of the dialogue between the two voices (a dialogue that is started by the piano, unlike what had always happened before in the genre «concert», in which the thread of the discourse was firmly held in the fist by the orchestra), for the anguish that emanates from the "questions" of the piano, for the inexorable responses of the orchestra. But then (and this is also a peculiar thing to note) the dualism hints at resolving in favor of the pleading voice because, towards the end of the dialogue, the orchestra's voice seems to soften its own hardness, it seems to tame and accept the requests of «begging principle». And, in fact, the second movement flows naturally, without interruption, in the third movement (an impetuous *Rondò*), which is a marvelous game of exchanges and pursuits between piano and orchestra, in a climate of joy that leads to a explosion of joyous brightness.

Fedele D'Amico correctly said that through the contrast and development, in the composition of Beethoven the return of the theme is not the recomposition of a symmetry, but a maturation: even if materially identical, the theme reappears matured and interiorly enriched; it's like to meet again an adult person known when he was young. This seems to me a very appropriate and effective image, which helps to penetrate the depth of Beethoven's music, to understand how Beethoven's inspiration is a powerful melting pot through which each theme matures and transforms itself.

The reference to the concerts for piano and orchestra leads us spontaneously, I would say almost necessarily, to mention the *Concert for violin and orchestra*, which is their brother. It is the op. 61 and is the only violin concert that Beethoven composed.

During Beethoven's life, this concert didn't get the fortune that the piano concerts received: at the point that Beethoven himself made a transcription for piano and orchestra, hoping to make it more popular. In fact, it is a concert that has a certain imbalance between the first movement, very vast and full of themes and brilliant solutions, and the other two movements, much more weak. But after Beethoven's death that violin concert took hold and became one of the highlights of violin literature.

This is a very beautiful concert, which opens with four mysterious, timed, charming kettledrum shots, and with a large orchestral introduction that prepares the entrance of the violin.

The first movement is set on two themes (someone lists three, considering a third theme what others consider as the "tail" of the second), both intensely lyrical, characterized by a relaxed *cantabile* that seems tailor-made for the violin. The weaving of musical discourse is complex, but always maintains characteristics of great and smiling sweetness. Beautiful, at the end of the cadence of the violin, the way the orchestra comes back, on a very long trill of the violin itself.

The second movement is a *Larghetto*, whose theme is immediately sung by the solo violin with the accompaniment of the muted arches, and then is taken up by horns, clarinets and bassoons. It is a calm and thoughtful movement; but soon it arrives at a *Fortissimo* which is a prelude to a brief cadence of the violin: this short cadence is the bridge that connects the second movement to the third one without a break in continuity. The third movement is a lively and wild *Rondò*. In this way Beethoven has merged the second and third movement in a single block that is opposed to the first movement and which rebalances the overall structure of the concert in two unique blocks.

Il Rondò is a delightful dance, which the violin's acrobatics make light and sparkling. It quickly rushes to the conclusion, through a cool and overwhelming dialogue between solo violin and orchestra.

THE «THIRD STYLE»

Beethoven's artistic itinerary is traditionally divided into three phases, to which the designation of "styles" has been attributed: the three styles of Beethoven. It is a somewhat elementary scheme that musicologists tend to overcome today. But it is a very useful reading key, which helps us to understand and orientate ourself in the vast and complex world of Beethovenian production. Allow me to use this key.

The first style is that of youth: an already personal style, but still linked to eighteenth-century schemes; it includes, basically, the period from 1782 to 1801.

The second style is that of the progressive affirmation of Beethoven's own personal way of composing and of his own very personal message: the message of the struggle between man and destiny, of «durch Leiden, Freude». It occupies, approximately, the period 1802-1815 and is the style in which the sonata-form finds its most congenial and most effective use (we said: the sonata as a drama). It is the season of the heroic, of the titanic.

The third style is the overcoming of drama, of titanism. It is the landing to a superior vision, of wisdom and of conquered humanity, to the equilibrium of those who have achieved joy and, in a certain sense, have overcome the dialectic of the opposites, composing these in a superior unity. It is the period 1816-1827. The sonata form, while constituting the essential mold in which the inspiration falls, loses the dualistic tension that characterized it, dissolves into a greater wealth of themes, reaches peaks of extraordinary simplicity and calmness. Mario Baroni told about a gradual transition from the level of conflict to that of a sort of contemplative fixity. Paolo Gallarati spoke of a new sound, in some way «perspective», which opens to the post-eighteenth century orchestra the magic of distance, resonance, and the sonorous shadow that extends behind the figure.

The three styles always find their first experimentation in piano music, then they pass into symphonic and chamber music. With a singular but effective comparison, Massimo Mila said that in Beethoven the piano sonatas are the assault troops, the symphonies are the occupation troops. In other words: Beethoven experiments with his "novelties" on the piano, then transfers them to the symphony.

The compositions that we have approached so far belong to the first two styles, and mainly to the second.

The third style finds its piano incarnation in the *Sonatas* op. 106, 109, 110, 111 and in the *Thirty-three variations on a waltz by Anton Diabelli* op. 120.

I recall in particular the gigantic *Sonata op. 106*, called *Hammerklavier* (which means "piano": almost to indicate that it is the piano sonata par excellence): it is an extraordinary synthesis of novelty and stylistic daring, which ends with a formidable three-parted fugue. But I would propose to listen, as a first step, to the *Sonata op. 101*, whose first movement immediately gives the measure of a pianistic world different from that of the previous style: instead of fight and contrast and drama, we find here calmness and reflexivity, a tender and mature sweetness, veiled with melancholy and distance.

Then the *Sonata op. 111*, the last one. Let's focus especially on the *Arietta*, which is the second movement: it begins with the enunciation of a theme that is a long distillate of rarefied simplicity and which then widens and becomes complex in a series of variations rich in originality, in which Beethoven seems to herald the developments of the music of the future (think that one of those variations prefigures the ragtime, that is the kind of rhythm that will become characteristic of jazz). The last variation explodes in an amazing cascade of trills, a shower of rutilant beauty at the end of which the initial theme of the *Arietta* reappears: but that theme comes back played by the right hand in the highest areas of the keyboard and accompanied by the left hand it plays in the lower, deeper areas of the keyboard itself.

The result is a strong tension, which has inspired Thomas Mann with a beautiful page of *Doctor Faustus*. That page highlights the enormous gap between the bass and the song, and he literally says: «There is a moment, an extreme situation in which it seems that the poor motive remains suspended, abandoned and solitary over a dizzying abyss». And when the theme returns, «it is the most moving, most consoling, most melancholic and conciliatory act that can be given. It is like a painfully loving caress on the hair, on a cheek, a last look in the eyes, quiet and deep». "Quiet and deep": it seems to me the most appropriate adjectival for this stage of Beethovenian art.

The succession of these sonatas, difficult to listen but beautiful, is a succession of unimaginable surprises, a journey into new and unexplored regions.

At a similar level the quartets of the third style are placed. These are works that can well be defined, Kantianly, transcendental. The thick and affable weaving of the quartet lends itself to meditative collections, to profound introspections. The delicate balances between the four instruments of this chamber formation (two violins, viola and cello) lend themselves to the flow of a calm, wise, intimate and serene discourse, above the fight and the agonistic commitment.

The quartet production of Beethoven develops along all three styles. The six quartets of op. 18 belongs to the first style; in the second style are put the three quartets of op. 59 (called *Rasumowsky Quartets* named after the dedicatee, the Russian ambassador to Vienna). The last quartets belong to the third style: those whose numbering goes from the op. 127 to the op. 135, passing through the numbers 130, 131, 132 and 133 (the latter is in the form of a fugue and is called *Grande fuga*).

We could listen to the *Quartet op. 132*. It was composed in the Spring of 1825, after a long illness: and of the illness it bears a visible and explicit trace. Beethoven himself gave the third movement this title: *Canzona di ringraziamento offerta alla divinità da un guarito, in modo lidico* (Canzona of thanksgiving offered to the deity by a healed, in a holistic manner). The "canzona" is developed on the basis of an alternation between ecstatic prayer and "return to life" full of joy for the regained health (in one point Beethoven has put the indication "feeling new strength"). On the naked and simple, almost Gregorian theme, prayer blossoms with a flowering of variations: a dense flow, a slow coloring of rich and expressive chords. I would say that in this prayer we must let ourselves be carried away by the flow of chords, each one tasting in their individuality, without the pretense of finding a precise melody.

After the fourth movement *Alla marcia, assai vivace* there is a poignant recitative, which introduces the last movement: a passionate *Allegro* in which themes of songs and dances are intertwined in a progressive crescendo that, with an epithet that I like a lot, has been called «Dionysian».

In the symphonic field belongs to the third style the *Ninth Symphony*, which we will describe in a separate paragraph. And next to the *Ninth* can be placed that other great vocal and instrumental masterpiece that is the *Missa solemnis* op. 123. It is not the only Mass that Beethoven composed; but it is certainly one of the highest points of Beethovenian art. At the beginning of the *Kyrie* sheet music of that *Missa* Beethoven wrote: "From the heart, can you again go to the hearts" ("Vom Herzen, möge es wieder zu Herzen gehn").

From this Mass I would invite to listen to the attack of the *Creed* (hammered with the strength of a convinced adhesion to the fundamental truths of the Christian faith); the *Sanctus* (punctuated by four slow beats played by a group of brasses); the famous *Benedictus* (with the celestial violin solo, in which the silence of the moment of the consecration of bread and wine - which is the focal point of mass according to the Catholic rite - is sublimated); and finally the *Agnus Dei*, with its war echoes that prelude the *Dona nobis pacem*.

NINE SISTERS

When you mention Beethoven, the thought runs spontaneously to his nine symphonies. Nine: a small number, if compared to the symphonic production of other composers (Haydn composed 107 symphonies, Mozart sixty). But this smallness has a precise meaning.

Massimo Mila uses an image that seems apt in his elementary evidence. He says: before Beethoven, writing a symphony did not cost the composer much; it was a bit like a chicken to make an egg: a daily task, a routine, an office job (apart from the last three Mozart symphonies); with Beethoven, instead, composing a symphony begins to become a fatigue similar to that of giving birth to a child.

Exact. It is no longer a matter of providing a good, harmonious and well-constructed product; it is a matter of expressing a message in which a life experience is concentrated and in which a need for communication is urgent: and then, the symphony becomes, as a child, a very original and unrepeatable reality.

And in fact, each of the Beethovenian symphonies has a very personal and unmistakable physiognomy: of these nine "sisters" each is a world unto itself, a compact, coherent, totally original universe. And therefore, in the course of these nine symphonies, the growth of the experience and the deepening of the message are captured. From a strictly musical point of view, for example, there is a noticeable progress in the transition from the first two symphonies to the third: there is a numerical explosion, since while the second symphony involves about forty performers, in the third the orchestra has almost doubled. Doubled, then, the power of sound, doubled the complexity of writing, doubled the wealth of instrumental timbre, intertwining, nuances. When we arrive at the *Ninth*, the staff expands further because the chorus is added to the powerful orchestra, with male and female voices, which are joined by the voices of solo singers.

I will dedicate the last paragraph to the *Ninth*; of the other symphonies I speak elsewhere in this chapter. Here we might try to listen, in immediate succession, to the *First* and *Third* symphonies (or the *Second* and the *Third*), focusing our attention on what has just been said. I have already spoken about the *Third*, but here I point out the last movement, which is dense with the richness of the themes, with their complex elaboration, with the variety of the tonal palette, with the fascinating singularity of the central theme. And I remember what Fedele D'Amico said very well: «A Beethoven symphony is neither broad nor narrow, neither long nor short, neither simple nor complex: it is a life-size organism in which the amplitude of the developments is organically homogeneous to the nature of the thematic material and vice versa». Of the nine symphonies, two are "sisters" in a very particular way: the *Seventh* and the *Eighth*. They were composed in the same period (1811-1812) and both are without a slow movement. Although the *Eighth* is considered "minor" compared to the *Seventh*, both come from the same creative impulse and share a joyful, "festive" nature. The whole *Seventh* has a fascinating beauty. Wagner saw the apotheosis of the dance and in fact it is the exaltation of the rhythm: from the first movement that opens with monumental "stairways and terraces" of notes, at the last movement when an overwhelming rhythm of bacchic taste is unleashed .

About the *Eighth*, Ernest Newman said that «it collects the overflowing of the mighty *Seventh*» in a «rush of joyful acceptance of life and the world». In that joyful acceptance there is also the joking parody of Mälzel's metronome, which I spoke about a while ago.

«YOU ARE THE BEST OF MEN»

In the last months of 1826 Beethoven had gone to the country by his brother Johann. He returned to Vienna in December, and made the imprudence of traveling on the milkman's open wagon. He took a pneumonia, then he had complications. The chronicles speak of dropsy; perhaps it was a pleurisy. He had a surgery to "remove water", but his health conditions did not improve, but worsened. However, suddenly after the surgery he felt a little better and, joking with the doctor, compared himself to Moses saved from the water. The strength of mind and humor accompanied him during the course of the illness. When he had some energy, he spent his time reading books and music scores.

His last weeks of life were illuminated by the presence of a ten-years-old, Gerhard von Breuning, son of his childhood friend Stephan von Breuning. From the conversation notebooks we get the constant, discreet and affectionate presence of this little boy, who encourages him, advises him, reminds him of the doctor's prescriptions, gives him the medicines, and is interested in his things and his readings.

It is a singular coincidence: in the Breuning family the boy Ludwig had made his first positive experiences, he was welcomed with esteem and affection, had his first contacts with the world of culture, and his personality had blossomed; and from the Breuning family, Beethoven, close to death, receives the gift of a delicate and wise presence, which offers him sincere and deep affection (the boy will say to him: «You are the best of men») and that satisfies his ancient and dissatisfied instinct for fatherhood.

Beethoven does not compose anymore. He no longer has the strength. But his art has now reached the goal of extreme simplicity. We have seen some examples of that in the *Sonata op. 111* and in the *Quartet op. 132*. We can also remember the *Bagatelle* op. 119 and op. 126.

It is interesting to listen to these piano works, to which Beethoven gave such a "disqualifying" title. "Bagatella" (or "bagattella") means "little thing", "thing of no value", "smallness". The German «Kleinigkeiten» means, in fact, «trifles». They are small things, in the sense that they are immune from titanicism, not in the sense that they are worth nothing. Instead they are worth much, because they are the ultimate distillation of a long and complex musical journey, in which simplicity and depth coincide. The discharged and confidential tone of the *Bagatelle* expresses a supreme freedom and draws on the deepest roots of man.

In March 1827 the disease worsened. When Dr. Wawruch saw that all hope of recovery was lost, he felt obliged to warn the patient: naturally in writing, with the usual system of conversation notebooks. The doctor tells:

«Beethoven slowly read the announcement with matchless firmness of mind, then remained somewhat thoughtful, while his face expressed great serenity. Affectionate and serious, he held out his hand to me, saying: "Send for the curate". Then he became silent and thoughtful again. Shortly afterwards he received the sacraments with the serenity of the Christian who looks in the face of eternity».

The reference to "the serenity of the Christian" is not a formula of use, a conventional phrase. Beethoven was really a convinced Christian, a man who - despite all his faults - had a profound sense of human and Christian values. His letters are littered with invocations to God, with a sense of prayer and adoration, of faith in the presence of God in human life. His references to the Gospel, and to the Bible in general, were frequent. On his table, among the familiar objects and the most loved books, was the *Imitation of Christ*, the famous work of a medieval mystic. For him, prayer was an essential act of the day. His fundamental optimism was born of two matrices that found an existential synthesis in him: the Kantian rationality and the gospel message of love.

Beethoven died on March 26th, 1827. A huge crowd participated in his funeral, mixing members of the Viennese high nobility and many humble people. They remember that an elderly woman, replying to someone asking her why so many people, said: «The general of musicians has died». Of those impressive funerals it was said: «Beethoven's death produced in Vienna an unprecedented emotion».

Almost an experimental proof of the universality of Beethoven's art, in whose music every human person finds something of himself.

In order to tune ourselves on the wavelength of that immense emotion, I would propose to listen to the second movement of the *Seventh Symphony*. It is not a funeral march; indeed, Beethoven called it *Allegretto*, which means "moderately lively". But, despite its rather quick rhythm, this passage is pervaded by intense emotion, a contained and strong sadness. In a symphony that is characterized by powerful pages (think at the beginning of the first movement, in which the orchestra moves majestically to successive waves, in a crescendo of ascending scales) and which has been called «apotheosis of the dance» for the rhythms very lively and almost orgiastic of the third and fourth movement, the *Allegretto* of the second movement is a parenthesis of recollection and pain: after a long, solemn and mysterious chord of the brass instruments, the violas and cellos, accompanied by the double bass, sing a simple and linear song, vibrant with infinite sadness; that song is spread over an evocative rhythmic accompaniment, and is taken over by the whole orchestra; then the melody is broken, shattered into sobbing pulsations; then it resumes its flow, but to end soon with the same mysterious chord with which the piece had opened.

LISTENING GUIDE TO A MASTERPIECE: THE NINTH SYMPHONY

The *Ninth Symphony* op. 125 is a very high expression of Beethoven's third style. It is the longest symphony, and it is the only one in which the human voice is used. This is a big news: a musical genre born for the orchestra expands, for the first time, to host the voices of soloists and choir. There is a precise reason: Beethoven considered the human voice to be the noblest instrument and the highest expression of music; for many years he wished to translate into music the *Ode to joy* by Schiller, a poem that Schiller had written in 1785 and which had a strong charge of humanity, optimism, and fraternity. The symphony is composed of four movements and has been defined as "the extraordinary flagship of modern western music". Massimo Mila has made a masterly analysis of it, to which I refer the reader eager to study. Here I just provide some ideas.

The first movement is an *Allegro ma non troppo*. It begins with a series of fragmented musical phrases: small descending snippets, inserted in a confused context that gives the sense of the indistinct and the unformed. A sort of chaos, from which soon the first theme emerges, net and imperious, of downward trend. It is a very effective opening, in order to which there are those who evoked the first page of the Genesis or the great Michelangelo's fresco of the creation of the world, to indicate the order that is imposed on chaos. A sweet and pastoral melody then introduces the second theme, which is, this time, an upward theme. An extensive development follows, in which the

168

techniques of variation and counterpoint are mixed, and the movement closes with a grandiose revival of the first theme.

The second movement is a very lively, in the form of a *Scherzo*. The *Scherzo*, in the symphonies of Beethoven, replaces what in the classical tradition of the symphony was the *Minuetto*, a typical aristocratic dance. It is a way to revolutionize the symphony, breaking the eighteenth-century schemes, while respecting the general structure of that type of composition. Here, however, the revolution is expanded, because Beethoven also innovates in the placement of the *Scherzo*, which passes from the third movement (which was in the aristocratic tradition) to the second movement, probably in order to insert a brisk and lively digression between the first movement, very long, and the third movement (which, as we shall see, is a long *Adagio*).

This *Scherzo* is a very animated, fast-paced, colorful, rhythmic by frequent interventions of the kettledrums and also by bass drum hits. It reminds a little of the *Scherzo* in the *Eroica* and has even vertiginous passages, against which it has been referred to the bacchic intoxication. And yet, even in that vertiginous whirlwind, this time is also strangely rich in pauses, long pauses, which give it a hesitant feeling: a bizarre contrast derives between the frenetic rhythm and the sudden silences.

After the whirl a delicate episode opens. It is the so-called *Trio of the ancient Minuet*. A sweet theme is sung by the oboe, then passes to the strings, then is taken up by the horns. It recalls some passages of the last movement of the *Pastoral Symphony*. And indeed there is a relaxed and pastoral climate. But then the initial swirling rhythm is resumed, and the movement runs to end with the full sound of a restless and unrestrained orchestra.

The third movement is a very and singable *Adagio*. In singular contrast with the aggressive and bacchic impetus of the previous movement, this movement is very slow and has induced critics to use the most colorful adjectives: celestial, sublime, empyrean, incommensurable... In fact, it is a page of supreme beauty and intense religious inspiration.

The first theme is entrusted to the strings, which are echoed by clarinets, bassoons and horns. It takes place with an ecstatic slowness. It is a calm, limpid meditation, imbued with an intimate peace. That theme is followed by another, slightly more moved. It is an *Andante* that enters with a rush and gradually takes altitude, with intense lyricism; it develops widely, often accompanied by a pinch of cellos and double basses; then it takes the way of variations. There are two variations that follow each other. Then an impetuous entry of trumpets and other brass instruments imposes and breaks the contemplation climate. The first theme, imploring, immediately reappears. But a second fanfare intervenes again, shortly thereafter. The strings seem to oppose to the fanfare, with the help of some brass intruments, in an attempt of resistance in which the second theme briefly flourishes. Then the movement "more than to conclude, goes out" (it is an expression of Mila). As if contemplation and peace (it has been said) were a too beautiful digression, destined not to last: a slightly pessimistic interpretation, which seems to me to be contradicted by the fact that this third movement is followed by the "movement of joy".

In fact the fourth movement can well be called the "movement of joy", being dominated by Schiller's *Ode to joy*. Beethoven chose the most significant verses of this hymn, leaving out those less happy and somewhat rhetorical.

The question arose of how to connect the human voice with the orchestral ensemble of the symphony. He had a long labor in this regard and then decided to leave the task of the junction to a baritone voice, making it say a phrase of invitation to the song, that is the passage from instrumental music to another type of music. But let's now see how this immense and complex last movement of the *Ninth* unfolds.

The beginning of the fourth movement shows a very clear separation from the previous movement. It is an abrupt and violent beginning, with very strong chords, supported by kettledrums and full of dissonances. Then the search for the theme of the *Ode to Joy* begins.

It is not out of place to talk about "research": the strong and solid voice of cellos and basses really seems to question what the most appropriate theme might be. Some fragments of the first movement emerge. But the orchestra shakes its head with a decisive "no" and discards the hypothesis. Some fragments of the very lively movement appear. But the orchestra shakes its head again and says another "no". Some fragment of the third movement is then sketched out, the *Adagio*. But here too there is the "no" of the orchestra: a "no" more tenuous than the previous ones, but still a "no".

For this beautiful passage the term "pantomime" has been used. I would say that it is appropriate, since it is really a sort of "gestures recital, without words". Naturally here the gestures are all exquisitely musical: but this does not detract anything from their plasticity.

And now the theme of the *Ode to Joy* is born: first with fragmentary hints, then gradually more delineated. The basses, after a long search, sketch it; and immediately it is resumed, in a whisper, from the cellos and bassoons, then from the

170

violins, in a crescendo in which it appears ever more clear, clear and defined. Now the whole orchestra plays it in a well-spoken and strongly rhythmic voice.

That theme has a martial trend, but it could not be called military; rather, it has a festive tone, which expresses a joyous and liberated fullness, as one who has found himself.

Some dissonances occur with the presentation of the theme, accompanied by kettledrums. They prepare the entry of the human voice. And this finally enters with a warm baritone tone, saying: «O Freunde, nicht diese Töne» ("Oh friends, no longer these sounds", we will sing, all together, more sweet and more joyful sounds). And immediately intones: «Freude!» ("Joy!"); the chorus promptly echoes: «Freude!» ("Joy!"). Then the first stanza of the Schillerian ode begins, with the words:

Freude, schöner Götterfunken, / Tochter aus Elysium, / Wir betreten feuertrunken / Himmlische, dein Heiligtum!
Joy, beautiful divine spark, daughter of heaven, we enter enthusiastically, or heavenly creature, into your sanctuary!

That stanza, intoned by the single voice, is immediately repeated by the choir. Waves of compact vocal and instrumental music follow, in which the choir sings:

Deine Zauber binden wieder / Was die Mode streng geteilt: / Alle Menschen werden Brüder / Wo dein sanfter Flügel weilt.
Your wonderful power reunites again what cruel costumes have separated: all men become brothers where your sweet wing rests.

A new episode is intoned by the quartet of soloists (soprano, tenor, mezzo-soprano, baritone), intercalated by the choir. It sings the joy of friendship, the joy of marriage, the joy of nature and of humanity immersed in it. In this song there is also a thought for those who live in solitude: a thought in which it is easy to glimpse a personal reference (reference in which the melancholy vibrates). Among those verses I remember:

Wem der grosse Wurf gelungen / Eines Freundes Freund zu sein, / Wer ein holdes Weib errungen / Mische seinen Jubel ein!
To those who had the great fortune to be friend with a friend, he who has obtained a gentle wife, join his joy!

171

The voices of the soloists come, in this episode, forced up to the spasm, so that someone has considered them unpleasant, but perhaps the unpleasantness is particularly linked to the sadness of the verses that say: «But who has never had this go away and leave in tears this assembly».

The next episode arises from a long pause of silence. It is intoned by the tenor with a sharp and impetuous voice:

Froh, wie seine Sonnen fliegen / Durch des Himmels prächt'gen Plan / Wandelt, Brüder, eure Bahn / Freudig, wie ein Held zum Siegen.
Happy, as its suns fly through the magnificent plains of the sky, follow, oh brothers, your way joyously, as a hero goes to victory.

They are very rhythmic verses, which lend themselves to a march. In fact, the music punctuates a small march, colored by the tone of the triangles and the plates.

Over this background the bold tenor voice is launched to celebrate the harmony of the stars and to invite men to translate this harmony into their cohabitation, with the joyful impetus of a hero who goes to victory.

The choir is associated with the tenor, with strong and pounding underlining of the word «Freude» («Joy»). Then tenor and choir are silent and leave the development of this joyful appeal to the orchestra. And the orchestra launches itself, in turn, into a large instrumental episode, in a fugato style, beautiful and overwhelming, in a crescendo of joyous pulsations. It is like a heartbeat, the heartbeat of joy: a universal, cosmic joy; the joy of living in the universe, but above all the joy of life of mankind. In this context, the mention of the "hero who goes to victory" acquires a profound innovative meaning: it replaces the hero-warrior who conquers victory with a new type of hero who identifies himself with the one who, spending his energies to promote human rights and to build the unity of the human family in justice, contributes to the victory of fraternity and peace.

Beethoven had already demonstrated this "planetary patriotism", an essential component of a "culture of peace", in the *Fantasia for piano, chorus and orchestra* op. 80, which already praised the peace and joy inspired by a text by Kuffner and in which - as Giorgio

Pestelli said, with a dense and effective expression, - «the fatherland is the whole man, sung by a citizen of the world». In the Schiller's image, taken over by Beethoven, there is therefore a significant overturning of the traditional "culture of war" in a "culture of peace".

The wide fugato closes with repeated chords in unison, which prepare the return of the chorus on the word *Freude* and on the first verses of the anthem.

Then, with a majestic surge of this sound mass, the choir intones with slow solemnity the verses that constitute the heart of the whole anthem:

Seid umschlungen, Millionen! / Diesen Kuss der ganzen Welt! / Brüder, überm Sternenzelt / Muss ein lieber Vater wohnen.
Embrace each other, oh millions of beings! This kiss, to the whole world! Brothers, above the starry vault must certainly live in a loving father.

I translated: "Embrace each other". But, properly, «Seid umschlungen» means «Be embraced», that is «Be united». This cry is repeated and developed in the following verses, and is sung with increasing register and intensity. The voices widen in a practically infinite number of sounds. On the words that go from "Brüder" to "wohnen" the voices are back in unison; but then they open again into a very wide range, which seems to embrace the whole universe. A music that has something cosmic, with acute vibrations, with very distant and mysterious echoes.
The «Muss» («Deve») is strongly hammered and developed with palpitant pulsations.

The last episode of the hymn resumes words and initial verses. The «Freude, schöner Götterfünken» is back, mixed with the repetition of the invocation «Seid umschlungen, Millionen». This mixture of verses is accentuated by the mingling of solo voices and choral masses. The piece reaches a point of maximum tension, in terms of speed, rhythm and intensity. And the orchestra closes and seals the whole with a series of very strong chords, in which the timbres of the piccolo, the plates and the kettledrums emerge very clearly.

The numbering of Beethoven's works that is commonly used is that proposed by Kinsky and Halm in their catalog. Substantially it follows the chronology of the compositions, albeit with some exception. It has now entered deeply into tradition and can be considered satisfactory.

The first readings that helped me understand Beethoven were: Romain Rolland, *Beethoven*, Rizzoli, Milano 1949 (later edited again by Passigli, Firenze 1984) and Antonio Bruers, *Beethoven, Catalogo storico-critico di tutte le opere*, Bardi, Roma 1950.

The Beethoven profile written by Romain Rolland is depicted with fervent interior participation and offers a vivid and fascinating image of the great composer. Bruers' catalog is very useful for orientating in the vast Beethovenian production: it is not only a dry list of works, as it provides a concise commentary of every work, and also contains very precious biographical notations. It has the defect of not being updated from the point of view of music criticism and often use excessively hagiographic tones.

Then I discovered Beethoven's epistolary in the edition by Alberta Albertini: *Beethoven. Epistolario*, Bocca, Torino 1947; and the book by Richard Specht, *Ritratto di Beethoven*, Garzanti, Milano 1947, a little fragmentary but full of news on the life of the musician.

A precious key to penetrate the art of Beethoven (as indeed that of any musician) is the *Breve storia della musica* by Massimo Mila, published initially by Bianchi-Giovini (Milano 1952) and the re-published by Einaudi, Torino. Mila then broadened his conversation on Beethoven writing the now famous *Lettura della Nona sinfonia*, Einaudi, Torino 1977. Mila himself recorded an Audiobook for Mondadori: *Per ascoltare Beethoven*, Mondadori, Milano 1978.

Extensive biographies are those by Walter Riezler, *Beethoven*, Rusconi, Milano 1977 e 1982; by Giovanni Carli Ballola, *Beethoven*, published in 1977 and 1979 by Sansoni/Accademia, Milano, and republished in 1985 by Rusconi, Milano; by Howard Chandler Robbins Landon, *Beethoven. La sua arte e il suo mondo in documenti e immagini d'epoca*, Rusconi, Milano 1997. More concise biographies, anyway sufficient to provide a comprehensive profile of the composer, are those by Gino Pugnetti, *Beethoven*, Mondadori, Milano 1965, and by Eduardo Rescigno, *Beethoven*, Fabbri, Milano 1979. Very good the *Beethoven* by Giorgio Pestelli, Il Mulino, Bologna 1988, including a very interesting collection of essays by various authors about the great musician.

I also recall: Luigi Ronga, *Bach, Mozart, Beethoven. Tre saggi critici*, Neri Pozza, Venezia 1956; Maynard Solomon, *Beethoven: la vita, l'opera, il romanzo familiare*, by Giorgio Pestelli, Marsilio, Venezia 1986; Guido Pannain, *Ludwig van Beethoven*, Arione, Torino; Gianfranco Zaccaro, *Beethoven o della sconvenienza*, Bulzoni, Roma 1979; Alfredo Casella, *Beethoven intimo*, Sansoni, Firenze 1981; Fedele D'Amico, *Beethoven*, Enciclopedia europea, Garzanti, Milano; Giorgio Pestelli, *L'età di Mozart e di Beethoven*, second edition, EDT, Torino 1991; Carl Dahlhaus, *Beethoven e il suo tempo*, EDT, Torino 1990; Giovanni Guanti, *Invito all'ascolto di Ludwig van Beethoven*, Mursia, Milano 1995; Maynard Solomon, *Su Beethoven. Musica, mito, psicanalisi, utopia*, Einaudi, Torino 1998; Franz Wegeler and Ferdinand Ries, *Beethoven. Appunti biografici dal vivo*, Moretti and Vitali, Bergamo 1999; Ugo Morale, *Introduzione a Beethoven*, Bruno Mondadori, Milano 1999; Piero Buscaroli, *Beethoven*, Rizzoli, Milano 2004.

Moreover: Philippe Antexier, *Beethoven: la forza dell'Assoluto*, Universale Electa/Gallimard, Trieste 1998; Stephen Kopfinger, *Beethoven*, Ricordi/LIM, Milano/Lucca 2006; Scott Burnham, *Il fattore Beethoven*, Enciclopedia della musica, by Jean-Jacques Nattiez, Einaudi, Torino 2004, vol. IV, from page 765; Benedetta Saglietti, *Beethoven, ritratti e immagini. Uno studio sull'iconografia*, De Sono/Tesi, Torino 2011; Von Paul Bekker, *Beethoven*, Schuster and Loeffler, Berlino/Lipsia 1912; Alberta Albertini, *Beethoven: l'uomo*, Bocca, Torino 1924; Otto Hellinghaus, *Beethoven. Memoria dei contemporanei*, Modernissima, Milano 1925; Edouard Herriot, *Beethoven: la sua vita e il suo tempo*, Tarantola, Milano 1947; André Boucourechliev, *Beethoven*, Editions de Seuil, Paris 1963; George Marek, *Beethoven: biography of a genius*, Kimber, London 1969; Maynard Solomon, *Il diario di Beethoven*, Mursia, Milano 1992; Hugo von Hofmannsthal, *Beethoven*, Graphos, Genova 1999.

About particular aspects of life and work I can suggest: Gilberto Todaro, *Il segreto e il messaggio della Nona sinfonia di Beethoven*,

Roma 1971; Martin Cooper, *Beethoven: l'ultimo decennio* 1817-1827, ERI, Torino 1979; Luigi Magnani, *Beethoven nei suoi quaderni di conversazione*, Einaudi, Torino 1975; Luigi Della Croce, *«Fidelio» di Ludwig van Beethoven: guida all'opera*, Mondadori, Milano 1983; idem, *Le nove sinfonie di Beethoven e le altre opere per orchestra*, Studio Tesi, Pordenone 1986; Giulia Giachin, *I Lieder di Beethoven*, Edizioni dell'Orso, De Sono/Tesi, Torino 1996; Gaspare Scuderi, *Beethoven e le sonate per pianoforte*, Muzzio, Padova,1985

About deafness and Beethoven's diseases I found useful the book by Luciano Sterpellone, *Pazienti illustrissimi*, Delfino, Roma 1985, pages 7-27; and the one by John O'Shea, *Musica e medicina. Profili medici di grandi compositori*, EDT, Torino 1991, pages 37-60.
Very interesting and moving are the memories written in mature age by Gerhard von Breuning, the boy who was close to Beethoven in the last weeks of his life: G. von Breuning, *Ludwig van Beethoven in my youthful memories*, SE, Milano 1990.

A monumental edition of the epistolary is the one edited by Emily Anderson, *Beethoven, Le lettere*, ILTE, Torino 1968.

Also scattered thoughts and diary pages are important. The latter are published by Maynard Solomon, in *L. van Beethoven, Autobiografia di un genio. Lettere, pensieri, diari*, Mondadori, Milano 1996.

For a general overview and an analysis of Beethoven's compositions you can see the vol. VIII of The New Oxford History of Music (translated into Italian by Feltrinelli and Garzanti, 1996).

For an interesting excursus on the diffusion of Beethovenian music in Piedmont we can consult Giorgio Pestelli, *Beethoven a Torino e in Piemonte nell'Ottocento*, Torino, Centro Studi Piemontesi, Fondo Carlo Felice Bona 1982.

I also point out that a large and interesting "notebook" on Beethoven and his time was published by "la Repubblica" as a supplement to n. 124 of the newspaper published on May 27th, 1987. Quirino Principe, Alberto Basso, Piero Rattalino, Claudio Casini, Giovanni Carlo Ballola, Maynard Solomon and other leading musicologists collaborated on it: it is a large, lively, interesting dossier that deserves to be consulted.

If you are particularly interested in the spiritual and religious issues concerning Beethoven, you will be able to find some indication in my book *Ascoltare l'Assoluto. Musica classica e annuncio cristiano*, third edition, Effatà, Cantalupa (TO) 2010, pages 69-151.